DEFINING
INFLUENCE

MACK STORY

ISBN: 0615996639
ISBN-13: 978-0615996639 (Top Story Leadership)

DEDICATION

To my wife Ria, my son Eric, and my mom JoAnne. I'm thankful you are taking the leadership journey with me. Each of you have made me better.

To Ria: You have been the wind beneath my wings lifting me higher than I could have ever gone without you. You're amazing. You're courageous. You're inspirational. Where would I be without you in my life? I love you pretty lady!

To Eric: You have impacted me in ways you will not understand until you have a child of your own. I'm proud of who you are and what you have accomplished. The future is yours. I'm excited to watch you grow. I love you buddy!

To Mom: You have always loved me unconditionally. You have always been there for me. You have never let me down. Watching you embrace leadership has been one of my greatest rewards. I'm proud of your growth. I love you Mom!

My life is much better because all of you are in it.

CONTENTS

ACKNOWLEDGMENTS

I would like to thank:

Don Large Sr., for seeing something in me when I didn't see it in myself;

Mr. Patel, for inspiring me to get a college education;

Jim Noreault, for giving me opportunities and modeling leadership for me and our team;

Zac Sharrow, for thinking of me and introducing me to Stephen R. Covey and *The 7 Habits of Highly Effective People*;

Elizabeth Mendez (Liz), for thinking of me and introducing me to John C. Maxwell, *The 17 Indisputable Laws of Teamwork*, and *The 21 Irrefutable Laws of Leadership*.

You all influenced my leadership journey. Without you having touched my life, I would not be who I am today or where I am today. I will always be grateful.

INTRODUCTION

When You Increase Your Influence, You Increase Your Options.

"Leadership is influence. Nothing more. Nothing less. Everything rises and falls on leadership." ~ John C. Maxwell

Everyone is born a leader. However, everyone is not born a high impact leader.

I haven't always believed everyone is a leader. You may or may not at this point. That's okay. There is a lot to learn about leadership.

At this very moment, you may already be thinking to yourself, *"I'm not a leader."* My goal is to help you understand why everyone is a leader and to help you develop a deeper understanding of the principles of leadership and influence.

Developing a deep understanding of leadership has changed my life for the better. It has also changed the lives of my family members, friends, associates, and clients. My intention is to help you improve not only your life, but also the lives of those around you.

Until I became a student of leadership in 2008 which eventually led me to become a John Maxwell Certified Leadership Coach, Trainer, and Speaker in 2012, I did not understand leadership or realize everyone can benefit from learning the related principles.

In the past, I thought leadership was a term associated with being the boss and having formal authority over others. Those people are definitely leaders. But, I had been missing something. All of the other seven billion people on the planet are leaders too.

I say everyone is born a leader because I agree with

1

John Maxwell, *"Leadership is Influence. Nothing more. Nothing less."* Everyone has influence. It's a fact. Therefore, everyone is a leader.

No matter your age, gender, religion, race, nationality, location, or position, everyone has influence. Whether you want to be a leader or not, you are. After reading this book, I hope you do not question whether or not you are a leader. However, I do hope you question what type of leader you are and what you need to do to increase your influence.

Everyone does not have authority, but everyone does have influence. There are plenty of examples in the world of people without authority leading people through influence alone. Actually, every one of us is an example. We have already done it. We know it is true. This principle is self-evident which means it contains its own evidence and does not need to be demonstrated or explained; it is obvious to everyone: we all have influence with others.

As I mentioned, the question to ask yourself is not, *"Am I a leader?"* The question to ask yourself is, *"What type of leader am I?"* The answer: whatever kind you choose to be. Choosing not to be a leader is not an option. As long as you live, you will have influence. You are a leader.

You started influencing your parents before you were actually born. You may have influence after your death. How? Thomas Edison still influences the world every time a light is turned on, you may do things in your life to influence others long after you're gone. Or, you may pass away with few people noticing. It depends on the choices you make.

Even when you're alone, you have influence.

The most important person you will ever influence is

yourself. The degree to which you influence yourself determines the level of influence you ultimately have with others. Typically, when we are talking about leading ourselves, the word most commonly used to describe self-leadership is discipline which can be defined as giving yourself a command and following through with it. We must practice discipline daily to increase our influence with others.

"We must all suffer one of two things: the pain of discipline or the pain of regret or disappointment." ~ Jim Rohn

As I define leadership as influence, keep in mind the words leadership and influence can be interchanged anytime and anywhere. They are one and the same. Throughout this book, I'll help you remember by placing one of the words in parentheses next to the other occasionally as a reminder. They are synonyms. When you read one, think of the other.

Everything rises and falls on influence (leadership). When you share what you're learning, clearly define leadership as influence for others. They need to understand the context of what you are teaching and understand they *are* leaders (people with influence) too. If you truly want to learn and apply leadership principles, you must start teaching this material to others within 24-48 hours of learning it yourself.

You will learn the foundational principles of leadership (influence) which will help you understand the importance of the following five questions. You will be able to take effective action by growing yourself and possibly others to a higher level of leadership (influence). Everything you ever achieve, internally and externally, will be a direct result of your influence.

1. *Why* **do we influence?** – Our character determines *why* we influence. Who we are on the inside is what matters. Do we manipulate or motivate? It's all about our intent.

2. *How* **do we influence?** – Our character, combined with our competency, determines *how* we influence. Who we are and what we know combine to create our unique style of influence which determines our methods of influence.

3. *Where* **do we influence?** – Our passion and purpose determine *where* we have the greatest influence. What motivates and inspires us gives us the energy and authenticity to motivate and inspire others.

4. *Who* **do we influence?** – We influence those *who* buy-in to us. Only those valuing and seeking what we value and seek will volunteer to follow us. They give us or deny us permission to influence them based on how well we have developed our character and competency.

5. *When* **do we influence?** – We influence others *when* they want our influence. We choose when others influence us. Everyone else has the same choice. They decide when to accept or reject our influence.

The first three questions are about the choices we make as we lead (influence) ourselves and others. The last two questions deal more with the choices others will make as they decide first, *if* they will follow us, and second, *when* they will follow us. They will base their choices on *who we are* and *what we know*.

Asking these questions is important. Knowing the answers is more important. But, taking action based on the answers is most important. Cumulatively, the answers to these questions determine our leadership style and our level of influence (leadership).

On a scale of 1-10, your influence can be very low level (1) to very high level (10). But make no mistake, you *are* a leader. You *are* always on the scale. There is a positive and negative scale too. The higher on the scale you are the more effective you are. You will be at different levels with different people at different times depending on many different variables.

Someone thinking they are not a leader or someone that doesn't want to be a leader is still a leader. They will simply remain a low impact leader with low level influence getting low level results. They will likely spend much time frustrated with many areas of their life. Although they could influence a change, they choose instead to be primarily influenced by others.

What separates high impact leaders from low impact leaders? There are many things, but two primary differences are:

1) High impact leaders accept more responsibility in all areas of their lives while low impact leaders tend to blame others and transfer responsibility more often.

2) High impact leaders have more positive influence while low impact leaders tend to have more negative influence.

My passion has led me to grow into my purpose which is to help others increase their influence personally and professionally while setting and reaching their goals. I am very passionate and have great conviction. I have realized many benefits by getting better results in all areas of my life. I have improved relationships with my family members, my friends, my associates, my peers, and my clients. I have witnessed people within these same groups embrace leadership principles and reap the same benefits.

The degree to which I *live* what I teach determines my effectiveness. My goal is to learn it, live it, and *then* teach it. I had major internal struggles as I grew my way to where I am. I'm a long way from perfect, so I seek daily improvement. Too often, I see people teaching leadership but not living what they're teaching. If I teach it, I live it.

My goal is to be a better leader tomorrow than I am today. I simply must get out of my own way and lead. I must lead me effectively before I can lead others effectively, not only with acquired knowledge, but also with experience from applying and living the principles.

I'll be transparent with personal stories to help you see how I have applied leadership principles by sharing: How I've struggled. How I've learned. How I've sacrificed. And, how I've succeeded.

Go beyond highlighting or underlining key points. Take the time to write down your thoughts related to the principle. Write down what you want to change. Write down how you can apply the principle in your life. You may want to consider getting a journal to fully capture your thoughts as you progress through the chapters. What you are thinking as you read is often much more important than what you're reading.

Most importantly, do not focus your thoughts on others. Yes, they need it too. We all need it. I need it.

DEFINING INFLUENCE

You need it. However, if you focus outside of yourself, you are missing the very point. Your influence comes from within. Your influence rises and falls based on your choices. You have untapped and unlimited potential waiting to be released. Only you can release it.

You, like everyone else, were born a leader. Now, let's take a leadership journey together.

Note: Chapters 16, 17, and 18 contain much of my personal transformation story that relates to my journey from front line factory worker to Lean Manufacturing consultant to Motivational Leadership Speaker and Author.

Some have said they would have liked to read those chapters at the start instead of at the end. Others have expressed they enjoyed reading them at the end. If you prefer to learn about much of my personal story and how I actually applied what I'll be teaching you before diving into the principles and the content, please go to those chapters first. Then, come back to Chapter 1.

Otherwise, it's time to dive in and learn how to increase your influence. And, you'll learn more about how I applied these same principles in my life as I share a bit of my personal journey with you in the chapters near the end.

WHY DO WE INFLUENCE?

1

LEADERSHIP

Defining Influence

"The key to successful leadership today is influence, not authority." ~ Ken Blanchard

Leadership is influence.

Merriam-Webster's definition of influence:
- the power to change or affect someone or something
- the power to cause changes without directly forcing them to happen
- a person or thing that affects someone or something in an important way

Let's look at all three definitions:

The power to change or affect someone or something – This is a very general context and covers all influence. You can influence with or without a position of formal authority. Formal authority is granted to you by others of higher authority. Your title, position, rank, etc. determine how much power you have over others through force or control, which is at best a very low level of influence. To the contrary, if you influence without formal authority, you are using moral authority and do not need to force or control others in order to influence them.

The power to cause changes without directly forcing them to happen – This definition is the primary focus of this book. In this context, you establish moral authority by adhering to self-evident principles applicable to all people and choose not to use formal authority, although you may have it. Stephen R. Covey, author of *The 7 Habits of Highly Effective People*, described moral authority this way, *"Moral authority is the gaining of influence through following principles."* Principles such as: fairness, respect, honesty, humility, gratitude, and courage. As you develop moral authority, your influence increases.

A person or thing that affects someone or something in an important way – In this context, power has been taken out of the definition. There is not a conscious effort based on power to influence. There is no moral or formal authority causing the influence to occur. At this level of influence, the *"person or thing"* is influencing purely by existing and the influence its existence has is very meaningful or *"important"* to those being influenced. A few good examples would be a book, a pet, money, a sentimental object, or an unborn or young child.

Consider the following question. At what point in your life do you begin to have influence? I am often asked, *"Are leaders born?"* My answer is always the same, *"Every single one is born."* This answer is poking fun at their question. What they are really asking is, *"Are people born with the ability to lead (influence) at a high level naturally?"* My answer is the same, *"Every single one of us is born with the ability to lead at a high level naturally."*

We are born with the freedom to choose. What we can or cannot do is ultimately based on our choices. We are born with different talents and more or less of a desire to lead (influence) at a high level, but we have the same *ability* to choose what we do, how we do it, and when we do it. What type of leader we are and what level leader we are is a primarily a result of our choices. Our leadership journey begins within.

The choices are the same for everyone. They may be harder for some and easier for others, but they are still choices. Understanding *leadership is influence* is vital to growing and defining our leadership. We have choices to make, and these choices determine how effective we are at getting the results we want. Our choices determine whether we will or won't lead at a high level.

If leadership in its most basic, generic form is simply influence, when does our influence begin? Here are a few common answers: *"When we meet someone." "When we start talking." "When we start a job." "When we finish college."*

Could it have been earlier?

When people begin to think deeply about influence, they quickly consider it starting early in their lives. Most people can trace their influence back to when they were born. But, ask yourself, *"Could it have been earlier?"*

If you have children, it's easy to help you understand when our influence begins by asking, *"When did your children begin to influence you?"* Most people with children instantly reply, *"As soon as we found out we were going to have a child."* If it's a mom, she says, *"As soon as I found out I was pregnant."* If it's a dad, he says, *"As soon as I found out I was going to be a father."*

Isn't that interesting? You were influencing others before you were born and without any effort. Your very existence in your mother's womb influenced the thoughts, emotions, actions, and choices of others.

You were not aware of it, but you had influence. Your parents started making decisions simply because you existed. Your existence established your influence. If you are a parent, this concept is easy to grasp and understand.

As you get deeper into this material, do not lose track of how much influence you have with others when they care about you. The more people care about you the more influence you have with them. It doesn't matter if they are your children, neighbors, co-workers, teammates, or boss.

The most important question to ask when it comes to influencing others is, *"Do they feel I sincerely care about them?"* People care about you more if they feel you truly care about them.

> *"Too often, we underestimate the power of a touch, a smile, a kind word, a listening ear, an honest compliment, or the smallest act of caring, all of which have the potential to turn a life around."* ~ Leo Buscaglia

The best way to begin to build influence is not to show others how smart you are or how much you know. It's to ensure, they feel without a doubt, you care about them and their future.

> *"No one cares how much you know until they know how much you care."* ~ Theodore Roosevelt

What motivates you more, how much someone knows or how much someone cares?

You were born a leader (person of influence). The instant you left your mother's womb, your natural actions were influencing those around you. It wasn't intentional. It was automatic. It was simply happening because you were here. You were simply trying to survive based on your natural instincts. Everyone in the room wanted to help you survive. You mattered then. You matter now.

People you had never met cared about you and helped you get started in this world. What character traits did they exhibit?

Many people have positively influenced us during various stages of our lives. When possible, we should personally thank them and let them know they made a difference. Each of them influenced us in various ways helping us become who we are today. We should be grateful they touched our lives.

Your awareness of self, others, and your environment has been increasing since your birth. It increased the most in your early years. For many people, it seems to slow down dramatically as they reach adulthood.

How much influence do you have with others at this moment? Your influence today is based on the choices you made in the past. Your influence in the future will increase or decrease based on the choices you make today.

Imagine how much potential influence you possess at this moment. How would your life change if your influence with others increased? To get to where you want to be in life, would it be easier with more or less influence?

Think of the choices you've made. Consider how all of them together have led you to the very spot you are today. Things outside of our control happen, but we are where we are today because of our choices. Our choices are within our control. It's easy to reflect when something goes wrong and say, *"If I had only done this or that, things would have turned out differently."*

Our choices matter not only today, but also tomorrow.

"A sign of wisdom and maturity is when you come to terms with the realization that your decisions cause your rewards and consequences. You are responsible for your life, and your ultimate success depends on the choices you make." ~ Denis Waitley

You may be thinking, what is the big deal with influence? The big deal is, unless you are going to live alone in an isolated place without other people, your influence with others is the key to your ability to live the life you want to live. You need others to help you get what you want.

"If you help enough people get what they want, they will help you get what you want." ~ Zig Ziglar

Ziglar had an uncommon way of thinking. He focused on helping others. Too many people simply want others to help them get what they want. No matter how you see it, you cannot help or be helped without influencing others. In order to help others, they must accept your influence. Or, if you want others to help you, you must be able to influence them to want to help.

Here is a simple example. Consider you are trying to get a new job along with 10 other applicants. Who will be selected? It will be the person with the most influence in these two areas: character (who they are) and competency (what they know).

Someone may think, *"It's neither of those things. It's who they know."*

Let's say it is because of who they know. What determined who they know? Their influence: character (who they are) and their competency (what they know). Therefore, we get the same answer. Their influence determines who they know.

Someone else may be thinking, *"The person they like the most is going to get the job."*

What determines that? Who they are and what they know.

Others may say, *"They select the person with the most education."* Maybe, but that's *"what they know."*

How we think and the choices flowing from our thoughts ultimately determine our level of influence with others. Our thoughts become the foundation for our choices. Our choices, all of them, determine whether or not we have influence with others and how much influence we have with them.

2

WHY DO WE DO WHAT WE DO?

Thought is the Foundation of Choice

"If you already knew what you need to know, you would already be where you want to go." ~ Mack Story

Merriam-Webster's definition of thought:
- an idea, plan, opinion, picture, etc. formed in your mind, something you think of
- the act or process of thinking
- the act of carefully thinking about something in detail
- a reasoning power
- the power to imagine

Your conscious thoughts are real but only in y*our* mind. They are within. Your thoughts lead to subconscious feelings or emotions. Once you act on your thoughts and feelings, they become choices. Choices allow your thoughts to become visible to others.

The Choice Formula:

Thought + Emotion + Action = Choice

Thought – something we are consciously aware of in our mind
Emotion – something we subconsciously feel based on our thoughts
Action – something we do

Your choices begin with thoughts. One choice you can make is to choose your thoughts. Just as there are strong and weak foundations, you can have strong and weak thoughts in your mind.

Our actions flow from our thoughts. The quality of the action depends on the quality of the thought. There is no conscious action without conscious thought.

Think of what your home looks like or think of your favorite car. Not only can you choose your thoughts, but as you just experienced, it is extremely easy for others to influence your thoughts. This is where our real problems start. Far too often, we accept the influence of others instead of rejecting it and using our own reasoning to determine our thoughts.

"Our mind may be likened to a garden, which may be intelligently cultivated or allowed to run wild; but whether cultivated or neglected, it must, and will, bring forth. If no useful seeds are put into it, then an abundance of useless weed-seeds will fall therein, and will continue to produce their kind." ~ James Allen

No matter one's intelligence level, we understand better and faster when we keep things simple. I like things to be simple. I grew up in a small, simple town: Tallassee, Alabama. The population is less than 6,000. But, I learned many valuable lessons there. One was to keep it simple.

I'll simplify Allen's words into my own. Our mind can be prepared to produce great thoughts and choices just as a freshly plowed field is made ready to produce a great crop. It can also be left undeveloped to produce whatever thoughts it may without any intentional intervention. But make no mistake, our mind will produce. Thoughts and choices will flow from our mind whether good or bad, beneficial or harmful. Sought or not, there is thought. Thoughts sprout from our mind as plants sprout from the earth. Abundantly.

When we garden, we are responsible for planting seeds capable of producing a great harvest. Likewise, we are responsible for developing our mind to produce great thoughts and choices beneficial to us, leading us from where we are to where we want to go.

We can take another step and work the garden continuously by watering, weeding, and fertilizing to ensure and enhance the quality of the crop. We can go farther in the development of our mind by associating with people who want to help us, by choosing to remove bad habits and toxic people from our lives, by intentionally studying how positive people think, by reading positive books, and by making positive choices. If we are getting good crops or good results, we can continue to work on getting something greater.

"We imagine that thought can be kept secret, but it cannot; it rapidly crystallizes into habit, and habit solidifies into circumstance." ~ James Allen

Discipline, or personal influence (leadership), is crucial in the decision making process. The actions flowing from the decisions materialize as choices. These choices will have positive or negative consequences.

One very powerful life and death choice is self-talk, thoughts we have about ourselves or others. Self-talk can create a wide variety of unpleasant circumstances if the thoughts are negative. Self-talk is also far more destructive than what others say to us or about us.

There are people taking their lives every day because of what they are saying to themselves, not because of what others are saying to them. Sometimes, they are not talking to others at all. Their thoughts have brought them to the point of feeling worthless, helpless, and worst of all, hopeless. Through self-talk, they have convinced themselves there is no reason to continue living.

"We must accept finite disappointment,
but never lose infinite hope." ~ Martin Luther King Jr.

These people no longer have hope. They have given up. When we don't have hope, we must get it from others. We must get around other people, be with them, and talk with them. We must borrow their belief in us. Others can and will lift us up.

If the people you are around won't lift you up, you are around the wrong people. The right people will always give you hope and lift you up.

The point of our thoughts creating our circumstances cannot be made clearer than this life and death example illustrates. There are endless examples of self-talk (thought) being detrimental to our well-being. We can choose our thoughts and change our thoughts. When we do, we change our habits and our circumstances.

"We are what we repeatedly do.
Excellence then, is not an act, but a habit." ~ Aristotle

Our thoughts form us, *who we are*, but we must first form our thoughts. Therefore, we decide who we are and the type of influence we have with others one thought at a time.

Once we start talking, the thoughts are no longer

thoughts. They are actions. They have materialized into a choice. We are interpreting our thoughts for others through spoken words and actions.

When speaking or acting, something very significant has happened. We are attempting to lead (influence) others intentionally. After speaking or acting, it's too late to decide if our influence we will be positive or negative. That should have happened while we were still thinking. Our intention is established in our thoughts and revealed through our words and actions.

Once we turn our thoughts into words, they will positively or negatively influence others. We can always pause and reflect in order to be sure the right words come out next time, but we cannot take them back once they are spoken. We can only influence the desired outcome by spending time intentionally thinking before we convert our thoughts into words.

There is something more influential than the words we speak when it comes to influencing others. It is our behavior. What do people see us doing? How do people see us living? Most have heard the old saying, *"Actions speak louder than words."* To put this into the context of this book, *"Actions influence more than words."*

This reminds me of an experience I had while helping John Maxwell make a difference in the country of Guatemala in June 2013. 150 others joined us. Together, we all trained over 20,000 Guatemalan leaders in just one week. John's mission was to initiate and lead the transformation of the entire country as they began to focus on becoming a principle-centered nation.

Most of us could not speak Spanish. Therefore, we had interpreters to help us conduct the training.

Bertha, my 20 year old interpreter, was talking with

me before one of our training sessions. She had obviously been reflecting on something I said during the taxi ride to the training site.

She looked at me and said, *"I don't know if I want to be a role model Mack?"* I said, *"Bertha you already are."* She looked at me in a puzzled way replying, *"I'm a role model?"* I continued, *"You're already a role model because someone is always watching you. You may not know it, but someone is always watching. And, when someone is watching you, you have the potential to influence their thoughts."*

She started to think about my words. I paused for a moment before saying, *"The real question you must ask yourself is not, 'Do I want to be a role model?' but rather, 'What kind of role model do I want to be?'"* This short conversation got her attention. My influence caused her to start thinking differently.

I have the power to influence. You have the power to influence. This book is all about the power of influence and helping others realize the ability they have inside to choose to be a powerful, positive person of influence. Our influence, positive or negative, comes from the inside and impacts the outside.

"If we are not modeling what we're teaching,
then we are teaching something else." ~ *Abraham Maslow*

We are not teaching what we are teaching. However, we are always teaching what we are modeling regardless of what we are teaching. Hopefully, we are in alignment and are modeling what we are teaching.

Have you ever told someone else not to do something you do yourself such as: unhealthy eating, risk taking, drinking, smoking, or using profanity? When we are saying one thing and doing another, we are out of harmony. We are not being congruent. It is very clear to others. We are being two-faced. We are not modeling what we are teaching.

How much real influence, without force, do you have? Should you have? Who are you? Do you live a life in harmony with the words you speak and the beliefs you hold? If not, does it matter to you? Until it actually matters, you will never change it. Saying it matters does not mean it matters. You must make specific choices to prove it matters.

If your thoughts are the foundation of your choices and your choices lead to your results, how much time are you spending thinking intentionally? When is the last time you spent 10 minutes a day consistently, day after day, week after week, intentionally thinking about how to get from where you are to where you want to be?

When have you done it for 90 days in a row? 60 days? 30 days? A week? Have you done it intentionally for 10 minutes at all?

I don't mean random thoughts while you have a minute or are driving along the highway. When is the last time you went somewhere quiet and thought: Who am I? Where am I? What are my circumstances? What do I want to change? What needs to change? How could life be better? What does it all mean? Why am I where I am in life? How can I change my circumstances?

This is significant. No matter where you are, you will not get from there to where you want to be without influencing yourself and others. If *you* do not change, *nothing* will change. Think on purpose: *Why do you want to influence* yourself and others?

What is the intent behind your thoughts?

3

WHY DO WE INFLUENCE?

Intent is the Foundation of Trust

"The key to good decision making is not knowledge.
It is understanding." ~ Malcolm Gladwell

Why do you want to influence others?

Those you are trying to influence want to know: What is your intent? What is your motive? What is your agenda? In other words, what thoughts are behind your behavior?

Our character determines why we influence. Who we are on the inside determines much of what happens on the outside.

Who are you? Really, who are you on the inside?

Who we think we are is important. Who we say we are is more important. But, who we really are is most important. Why do we do the things we do? Why do we say the things we say? Who we are is revealed to others by our thoughts, choices, and the intent or why behind them all.

I'm sure you already know, first impressions are extremely important. When it comes to character, our intention is our first impression.

What we do and say builds trust or creates distrust. This is important because trust is the foundation of influence. But, what is the foundation of trust? It is the why behind everything we do and say. Intent is the foundation of trust.

From time to time, I will begin asking thought

provoking questions to help you *"Stop and Think."*

After you have thought about the question from your own perspective, turn it around and ask it from another's perspective assuming you are on the other side of the question. Don't forget the importance your thoughts have on the choices you make.

You can increase your influence with others which will increase your effectiveness. The questions I ask will help you determine if your influence with others is increasing or decreasing based on the principles being discussed. The questions are presented from your frame of reference looking outward at others because when it happens to you, you not only see what is happening, but you also feel what is happening.

When you try to look at a situation from another's perspective, you usually continue to see and feel from your own perspective. Unless you are extremely good at empathizing, seeing and feeling how others see and feel, you may find it difficult to truly see things from another's perspective. You can and should learn this valuable connecting skill.

Let's give it a try as we start discussing intent as the foundation of trust.

Stop and Think: When someone builds trust with you, does their influence increase or decrease?

Everyone says, *"Influence increases."* It is a self-evident truth. The more we trust someone, the more influence they have with us. It is a natural law, a principle. Greater trust means greater influence. Therefore, when we build trust with others, our influence increases with them. It works both ways.

Stop and Think: When someone creates distrust with you, does their influence increase or decrease?

Everyone says, *"Influence decreases."* It is another self-evident truth. The less we trust someone, the less influence they have with us. The more others distrust us, the less influence we will have with them.

As self-evident truths, everyone always knows the answer to both of the previous questions.

The principles of trust are directly related to establishing influence. Be sure you internalize this principle before moving on. There is more detail on trust in later chapters, but it will help you now if you have the basic understanding of the impact trust and distrust have on your influence.

Why is there so much distrust in our lives, in our families, in our workplace, in our government, in general all over the world? It comes down to why we do what we do and why others do what they do.

The intent behind what we do transfers to others. They can see it. They can feel it. We cannot hide our intent. We also shouldn't need to hide it.

Everything we do and say has the potential to influence others. But, why do we actually do what we do and say what we say? Why we influence others, our intent, comes down to two complicated reasons that seem rather simple at first: manipulation and motivation. There is a very fine but important line between these two words.

When we are manipulating someone, we are using our influence primarily for our benefit. When we are motivating someone, we are using our influence for mutual benefit. Both parties get something out of it. There is a valid reason for both of us to take action.

Merriam-Webster's definition of manipulation:
- to control or play upon by artful, unfair, or insidious means especially to one's own advantage

The key component of this definition is *"especially to one's own advantage."* When you are using your influence to manipulate someone into doing something, only you receive advantage or benefit.

Stop and Think: When someone attempts to manipulate you, do they build trust or create distrust? Do they have more or less influence?

Merriam-Webster's definition of motivation:
- the act or process of giving someone a reason for doing something

The key component of this definition is *"giving someone a reason for doing something."* When you are using your influence to motivate someone to do something, there is mutual advantage or benefit. A reason or benefit not only for you, but also for them.

Stop and Think: When someone motivates you, do they build trust or create distrust? Do they have more or less influence?

When you believe, *"I'm here to serve others."* you begin to motivate others. You move others to action. However, when you believe *"Others are here to serve me,"* you begin to manipulate others.

High impact leadership is about motivation. Low impact leadership is about manipulation. Which person has better intent: someone wanting to serve others or someone wanting to be served by others?

Who decides if something is an advantage or benefit for you? You do. How can someone else truly know what is valuable to you at any given moment based on the circumstances in your life? They can't.

Likewise, you don't get to decide if someone else is benefiting or gaining an advantage. They do. They decide if there is a reason for them to act, not you. It makes perfect sense to me. How about you? I decide for me. You decide for you. Pretty simple.

However, we must realize that what may be motivation for one person may be manipulation to another person because people are different and have different values.

Different people live with different circumstances in their lives. We have different relationships with different people. Different people see things differently based on where they are and where they have been. They have different views of the world. People see the world as they are, not as it is.

Every relationship we have is different. There is no cookie cutter, one size fits all approach to influence. To be an effective leader (person of influence), we must be dynamic while learning and applying leadership principles.

Many people do not understand or have not considered the difference between principles and practices and run into trouble as a result. A principle can be applied in any situation and will deliver consistent results. A practice can be applied in any situation too, but there is a very big difference. A practice will not produce the desired results in any situation. Practices only produce the desired result in

HOW DO WE INFLUENCE?

4

FOCUS ON BUILDING TRUST

Trust is the Foundation of Influence

"Trust is the one thing that changes everything."
~ Stephen M. R. Covey

Our *intent* can potentially provide the foundation upon which we can start building trust. If we have the right *intent* behind our influence, we will have a strong, solid foundation. One not easily damaged. One sustainable during times of adversity. Although trust may be broken, we have a much better chance of rebuilding trust on a strong, solid foundation.

Having a strong, solid foundation of intent is necessary, but it is not enough. We must build tall and strong walls of trust allowing positive influence to flow from the inside while keeping negative influence on the outside.

Trust is the foundation of influence. Without trust, there is no influence. Without influence, there is no relationship. Without strong, solid, and meaningful relationships, we become extremely limited.

Our methods of influence determine how we build our walls of trust. While in Guatemala with John Maxwell, we taught that 87% of our influence comes from our values, our consistent actions, and our ability to work well with others. In other words, our character or who we are. Only 13% of our influence comes from our technical skills, abilities, and knowledge. In other words, our competency or what we know.

The evidence to support this is everywhere we look.

*"We get hired for what we know, but we get fired
for who we are." ~ John C. Maxwell*

The principle found in John's quote applies to personal relationships too. The words would be slightly different: We get accepted for who others *think* we are, but we get rejected for who we *really* are.

How many times have you met someone in your personal life or witnessed someone come into an organization and think *"they are great"* only to get to know them over the next few weeks or months and find yourself thinking *"they are not so great."* Who we are matters. Who we are on the inside determines where we go on the outside.

Without question, our potential to work with and through others is directly related to our influence. Therefore, the majority of our influence comes from our character (who we are) while only a small amount of our influence comes from our competency (what we know). Without a high level of influence, we limit ourselves. To get great results, we must not only motivate ourselves to action, but we also need others to help us along the way. The quality of those who decide to help us depends on the quality or level of our influence. It starts with us. We must go within, or we *will* go without.

How we influence is determined by our character combined with our competency. When looking at the building blocks of trust, the focus should be primarily on building our character and secondarily on developing our competency. Our character is constant no matter the situation. However, our competency is situational meaning trust can only be built in this area when our competency aligns with the demands of a specific situation.

Who we are and what we know combine to create our unique style of influence which determines *how we influence* others. We can always improve our style, and we can always change our style.

Every time we interact with someone, we are either building trust or creating distrust, not only with them, but also with everyone watching or listening.

> *"The most important thing in communication is to hear what isn't being said."* ~ Peter Drucker

What we see and feel builds trust or creates distrust. As time passes, people will either trust us more or trust us less based on all of our interactions. Trust does not just happen. We must be intentional if we are to be successful at building high trust relationships.

> *"When building rapport, we are conveying to others, I'm like you, so it's okay for you to like me."*
> ~ Christian Simpson

When building rapport, we relate to and connect with others by being like them. This allows them to feel safe to open up and connect with us. We can talk like them, dress like them, act like them, use the same language, etc. Doing so helps and is important.

The foundation of rapport is *sincerely caring for the other person.* Intent is the key. There is no better way for us to say, *"I'm like you, so it's okay for you to like me,"* than to honestly, openly, genuinely, and authentically care for someone.

We know the other person cares about themselves, but not necessarily in a prideful, ego-driven way. Hopefully, they genuinely care about and value themselves in a healthy manner with humility as we all should. When others feel we care about them, they do not question our intent.

Stop and Think: If someone does not care about you, but they are trying to influence you, what is their intent?

Once they know we care about them unconditionally, they do not care how we dress, what we look like, what we sound like, how big or small we are, or how tall or short we are. People connect deeply and quickly with people who care about them.

The best connectors are people who genuinely care about all people, not some people. It comes through almost instantly. You feel it when you meet them. They have the *"it"* factor when it comes to building rapport because they really do care.

The stronger our rapport is with people, the easier it is for us to build trust into the relationship. Trust is pretty easy to understand on the surface, but it gets complicated when you start to break it down into components.

When we build trust, we are doing something for someone to demonstrate we value them or want to add value to them. We make them feel good, make their life easier, show we care, or help them. We can feel when trust has been or is being built.

Building trust may be something as small as giving someone a pat on the back, calling someone by name, showing gratitude, or smiling. Or, it could be as large as buying someone a new car, a home, or sending them on an all-expense paid vacation. It could be listening when they need someone to talk to, believing in them when they don't believe in themselves, preparing a meal for them, mowing their lawn, washing their car, or acknowledging their children.

We should not make deposits of trust in order to take withdrawals of trust. Our ultimate goal should be to never create distrust, but we will. Our goal should be to keep building trust intentionally to strengthen our relationships over time.

Creating distrust is easy to understand. If you are like most people, you usually recognize when someone creates distrust faster than you notice when someone builds trust. Distrust is typically more strongly connected to our emotions, and we usually feel it instantly when it happens. When we are creating distrust, we are being disrespectful, devaluing others, causing others physical or emotional pain, making their life harder, and causing them to question if we truly care.

Creating distrust could be something as small as not saying thank you, ignoring someone when they walk in the room, or not waving or saying hello as we pass in the hallway. Or, it could be as big as causing someone bodily harm, stealing from them, yelling at them, or hurting someone close to them. It could be talking about them behind their back, not listening, rolling your eyes when they speak, making a joke about them, or taking credit for something they did.

We will also create distrust accidentally or automatically at times. The more time we spend with someone the more distrust we create. We may or may not know we have done it. Make no mistake, it is happening. If we do not become intentional about building trust, we risk losing trust.

Understanding accidental or automatic distrust is extremely important. We often spend more time personally with those we are closest to and care about the most or professionally with those in a position to help us the most.

We must offset the accidental or automatic distrust created with *intentional* efforts to build trust. Otherwise, we will end up in a relationship where there is more distrust than trust. What does this look like in our personal lives? Divorce, separation, ruptured relationships with those closest to us, or hard feelings. What does this look like in our professional lives? Terminations, layoffs, reprimands, demotions, pay cuts, lost responsibilities, stagnation, or hard feelings.

You can validate this principle of accidentally or automatically creating distrust. Think of a strong relationship you have with someone you don't see very often like an old high school or college classmate, a friend or relative living far away, someone you were in the military with years ago, or a former co-worker. Any of these types relationships can be used to validate this principle as long as there was strong trust when the separation happened.

How is it when you see them again? Everything is still great. It's like you haven't missed a beat. It's just like old times. It's this way because you have not been around each other to create distrust automatically. The trust built before is still there.

When someone does something nice for you and you don't appreciate it, you are creating a small amount of distrust. Or worse, you get used to them doing it, take it for granted, and feel entitled as though it is their job to do nice things for you. If this is the case, you are automatically creating large amounts of distrust on a regular basis.

Ria has done the cooking from the very beginning of our relationship. She loves it, and she is good at it. She knows how to prepare a meal. I'm not good at it. But, let me tell you what I am good at: appreciating it every time. I would never tell her to cook all the time, and I definitely would never expect her to cook all the time. Telling or expecting people to serve you always creates distrust even if you do appreciate it. There are endless examples at work and at home where we have the choice to either build trust or create distrust with others.

For a relationship to exist, both people must feel more trust than distrust. If either person feels more distrust than trust, the relationship will soon be over. Actually, it already is over. It's just not official yet. Both parties in the relationship need to be aware of this principle. It's good if at least one is aware, but it's great if both are aware.

5

EVALUATE YOUR EXPERIENCES

Reflection is Looking Backward to Go Forward

"By three methods we may learn wisdom: First, by reflection, which is noblest; second, by imitation, which is easiest; and third by experience, which is the bitterest."
~ Confucius

Experience is not the best teacher. Evaluated experience is. Our biggest mistake is not the mistake we made. It's not learning from the mistake. In order to learn from our past and move forward, we must reflect on our mistakes by evaluating the choices that led to the mistake. What did we not do? What should we have done? What could have been different? What do we need to do differently next time?

Others evaluate our intent based on *why* they feel we are trying to influence them. This happens consciously and subconsciously. Our intent is something we get to choose. Our character is revealed by our choices, and this is how others learn who we are. Who we are matters. Our intent matters.

Others decide how we make them feel, not us. We only influence. We don't determine. However, we can change the *why*, the intent, behind our influence in an attempt to get different results.

The best way for me to illustrate how looking backward can help move us forward is to share a few examples from my life.

As I transitioned from a *"me"* mindset to a *"we"*

mindset, which included intentionally helping and valuing others, my world began to change. In my early twenties, I worked long hours, so I could have more things. When I was not working, it was still about me. Everyone knew it except me.

"Narcissism falls along the axis of what psychologists call personality disorders, one of a group that includes antisocial, dependent, histrionic, avoidant and borderline personalities. But by most measures, narcissism is one of the worst, if only because the narcissists themselves are so clueless." ~ Jeffrey Kluger

I spent my time hunting, fishing, and unfortunately partying and hanging out with people like me. People going nowhere. They didn't care, and I didn't care. I thought I was doing well. I had a job and was paying the bills, sometimes not as easily as others. I just wanted to have fun.

They were happy coasting through life, and I was happy coasting through life. So, we coasted like many people still do every day.

Reflecting and thinking about my past reminds me of the scene in *Alice in Wonderland*, by Lewis Carroll, where *"Alice came to the fork in the road. 'Which road do I take?' she asked. 'Where do you want to go?' responded the Cheshire Cat. 'I don't know,' Alice answered. 'Then,' said the Cat, 'it doesn't matter.'"*

We were not thinking about what we could do. We were complaining about what we couldn't do. My influence was high but on the negative scale. My influence was used mostly to waste people's time and money, as I was wasting my own. There is nothing glorious about wasting time. People who waste their time won't mind wasting yours. I had natural leadership, and it was easy to influence those around me.

Who was I influencing? People on the negative scale with me. People like me with little, if any, positive influence with those getting results and making a positive difference in the world. My influence was with people going through the motions day in and day out. Week in and week out. Those trying to *"get by"* as we used to say. We were headed in no specific direction.

The intent behind my influence was wrong. It was about me. It was about having fun whenever there was time available to waste. It was not about helping others succeed and advance which would have started with helping myself succeed and advance. It was about living the status quo while settling and coasting through life.

As long as I was happy with *my* results, nothing else mattered. Sadly, I didn't care or have any concern for others, even those closest to me. Worrying about myself and no one else was an easy life. It wasn't very rewarding, but it was easy. I was going through the motions always looking to escape but not having a clue about how to do it. I also wasn't associated with anyone with a clue. I was not taking responsibility for myself much less anyone else.

No one I trusted knew about leadership as I understand it today. I had not heard of Stephen Covey, John Maxwell, Les Brown, Napoleon Hill, James Allen, or any of the other popular leadership experts. At my level of awareness, leadership was not on my radar.

Relative to our character (who we are), we attract people like us. We are also attracted to people like us. Although I didn't realize I was clueless, I also didn't realize those around me were too. I was subconsciously attracted to people like me. At that level of *"unawareness,"* our subconscious takes over. I was clueless and attracted to other clueless people.

I hung around people with small minds, like me. Therefore, I remained small. I hung around reactive people, like me. Therefore, I remained reactive. I hung around people without a vision, like me. Therefore, I didn't develop a vision.

Too many people want different results, but continue to be the same person and hang around the same crowd. They get stuck hanging with people with the same *why* behind their influence, those with the same general intent and similar character. Generally, they also influence people for the same reasons at the same level.

However, their competencies (what they know) can be much different. To illustrate, consider the work you do. Think of your co-workers or teammates. Although their competency is basically the same, they don't all socialize together. They are attracted first to those with similar character. A person's competency is usually an afterthought unless you are working on something together.

The issue of competency comes in a distant second and usually does not matter at all. Often, you see groups of people with totally different backgrounds hanging out on a regular basis. Character matters most when it comes to those we are attracted to or those attracted to us. If we want to change who we attract, we must change our character. None of the other seven billion people on the planet can do this for us. Only we can change ourselves from the inside out.

If we want to be around people with a higher level of influence than those we are currently associating with, we must raise our level of influence. How do we increase our influence? We go within. We work on *why* we want to influence ourselves or others, our intent. When we work on our character first, we cannot lose. Most people seek more competency when they can't get ahead in life. Developing competency is easy. Working on your character isn't easy. It's hard.

For me, working on my character meant getting control of myself first. I was a very reactive person. I was short tempered. I took stupid risks. I did stupid things because it was fun. I was impatient. I blamed others.

I did things which proved to the world I could not control myself while thinking I was in total control. I was doing many things a responsible proactive person would never do. I did some things right, but I did many things wrong.

Stop and Think: Do you trust people with self-control more or less than you trust people without self-control? Which person has the most influence?

Why would we trust someone without self-control? We shouldn't. No one should trust them based on their lack of control. We wouldn't know what we were going to get or when we would get it. These people are unstable. I used to be unstable until I heard Stephen R. Covey in 2008, say, *"Between stimulus and response there is a space. We can use this space to choose our response."* His words changed my thinking which allowed me to transform my life.

When I heard those words, I immediately started reflecting and couldn't believe how blind I had been. I was beginning to look back to go forward.

I had never considered that principle. My life was about to change dramatically for the better. I had no idea the impact learning, applying, and beginning to live that principle would have on my life. It led me to write this book six years later.

When I heard Covey say those words, my son, Eric, was 17. Our relationship had been nearly non-existent for the past two years, and it would be another two years before I had done enough work on myself to regain influence with him. My relationship with my Dad had been nearly non-existent for over 20 years. Needless to say, Covey had my attention.

I fixed the problem. ME! Those relationships have been mended. Eric and I are now very close, and I talk with Dad more often.

Covey's words dramatically influenced my life. The principle of being able to choose my response to any stimulus was then, still is, and always will be *the foundation* of my leadership journey. Leadership principles are real and produce the desired results. I hope something on these pages inspires you to make improvements in your life too.

My life literally improves daily as I continue my personal growth journey. I am ready to extend my influence beyond my current reach with hopes of helping others grow their leadership (influence). This is my first book and is a big part of my journey. It is a natural next step. I am excited to be writing it and know it will help people get better results. Unfortunately, I will never meet most of them.

One thing to consider is the reaction of those around you as you grow. Make a mental note; average people want to keep you average. Not because they are bad people, but because they want you to remain like them and with them. Sometimes, those trying to hold you back are those closest to you such as family, friends, co-workers, etc. It won't take long before you start to hear comments like these. *"You never come around anymore." "You think you are better than us." "You think you're too smart to hang around with us."*

Tell them, *"I don't think I'm better than you. I'm not. It's like this. If you are heading to LA and I am heading to New York, I'm not riding with you. Not because I'm better than you, but because I am going in a different direction."*

As you grow, you must leave some people behind. They may not be going where you're going. They make their choices, and you make yours. You may influence them to grow with you. If not, you cannot stay with them. You must move forward on your journey. Most people can relate because they have already left people behind in their lives to be where they are now. This must happen when growth happens.

You cannot and should not depend on others to motivate you. If you are depending on others to motivate you, you are already in trouble. Most often, others won't motivate you. Part of taking responsibility for yourself and leading yourself is motivating yourself.

Nothing will motivate you more than finding your purpose. Finding your purpose begins with finding your passion. If you follow your passion, it will lead you to your purpose.

Stop and Think: Who would you trust more to come through for you? Someone lazy and unable to get themselves going? Or, someone who is self-motivated? Which one would have more influence?

Do yourself a favor as you read: take time to reflect and ask yourself how you're doing on the principles you are learning about.

DEFINING INFLUENCE

"The quality of a person's life will always be in direct proportion to the quality of questions that person is willing to ask themselves." ~ *Socrates*

I hope you reflect on the words from Socrates for a moment before continuing. What questions are you asking yourself while you're reading? Are you reflecting on your thoughts and choices?

Having an experience does not automatically result in learning. If we want to learn from an experience, we must be intentional and reflect on and evaluate the experience in order to pull out the lessons.

Apply the principle of reflection to learn from experiences, especially mistakes. Making the mistake is bad enough. Not learning from it is worse because we will likely make it again. If we do not learn from our mistake, we simply had an experience; but we haven't gained experience.

Reflection alone is not enough. In order to gain value from reflecting, we must take action and make changes. What matters most is not what we are thinking about changing, but what we are actually changing.

6

LEAD YOURSELF FIRST

Respond Based on Values not Feelings

"The first and best victory is to conquer self." ~ Plato

Before you can motivate and grow yourself, you must control yourself. The hardest work you will ever do is on you.

The only person you have 100% control and influence over is you. However, doing the right thing at the right time is often much easier said than done. Some things say easy, but do hard. When I finally slowed down enough to realize I was involved in every problem I ever had, I truly discovered what needed to change most: ME!

Playing in my head when I made this discovery were the words, *"Between stimulus and response there is a space. We can use this space to choose our response."* I was slowly but surely becoming proactive. When we choose to be proactive, we are choosing to respond based on values that are aligned with natural laws and principles. We do not respond based on our feelings.

To understand what it means to be proactive, it's helpful to understand what the opposite of being proactive is. It is to be reactive. When we are reactive, we choose our response based on the feelings we have at the moment instead of values that are aligned with natural laws and principles.

There are always two ways of dealing with the same problem. Be proactive or be reactive. Each way will produce a different and natural consequence. Being proactive will make things better. Being reactive will make things worse.

Being proactive can change your life for the better if you fully understand and apply the associated principles. The more you apply them, the better your results will be. The less you apply them, the worse your results will be. You have already been proactive whether you knew it or not. Whenever you made choices that improved relationships, added to your success without trampling, devaluing, or taking away from others, or caused you to be effective rather than ineffective, you have been proactive.

An easy to understand physical law is gravity. Everyone understands the natural law and principle of gravity and how it works. It's easy to see it in action, and it's easy to prove the consequences of being aligned with or being out of alignment with this principle.

For example, you could choose to stand on the top edge of a thousand foot tall vertical cliff like those alongside the Grand Canyon. Being in alignment with natural laws and principles will ensure you remain safe and enjoy an awesome view of the canyon. You could also attempt to defy the law of gravity by stepping off the edge of the cliff. But, the law of gravity will determine your natural consequence, not you. You would immediately make your way to the bottom of the canyon. The outcome would be the same whether you chose to believe in gravity and whether you didn't.

We have 100% control of our choices. No one can ever take away our freedom to choose our response when something happens. We choose our actions, but natural laws and principles will always determine our consequences.

Physical laws and principles are much easier to see and understand than the psychological laws and principles which guide human interaction. But, these psychological laws can still be seen, felt, experienced, and they are self-evident.

In 2006, Ria and I purchased Eric an extended cab four wheel drive truck for his 15th birthday to reward him for his outstanding academic accomplishments. He had made all A's and only three B's since starting kindergarten. We planned to let him learn to drive it for a year while he had his learner's license before we handed him the keys at age 16 when he would officially be able to get his driver's license and drive alone.

Shortly after getting the truck, Eric made a poor choice. At age 15, he chose to sneak his mother's car out of the garage one night while everyone was sleeping and drive 25 miles away to hang out with his friends in a nearby town. His mother and I had divorced when he was five years old.

I immediately over-reacted and took his truck away. To make it clear he wouldn't be getting it back, I traded it in on my dream car, a 2003 Corvette Z06. His poor choice was followed by another poor choice on my part. I didn't know then what I know now. I chose to be reactive based on feelings and misaligned values.

I definitely overreacted. This one poor choice ruptured my relationship with Eric. I would continue to make many poor choices that ensured our relationship remained ruptured for the next four long years.

I should have considered his track record, the overall situation, and many more variables. However, I didn't pause to reflect on those things. I simply reacted based on my feelings. Unfortunately at the time, I valued control more than I valued our relationship. I would give anything to relive those years with Eric, knowing what I know now. That isn't not possible, but helping others learn from my mistakes is possible.

A year later when Eric turned 16 and received his driver's license, my mother chose to give him her car. We had planned a vacation to Panama City Beach, FL at about the same time and invited Eric and one of his friends to go with us. He accepted because we were going to allow him to experience more freedom and responsibility by allowing him to follow us in his car on the way down. It would be his first road trip behind the wheel of his own car.

Eric had his new found freedom thanks to my mother's generosity. Ria and I gave him permission to drive his car with the understanding that he would not be driving it at night when the partying and drunkenness was happening along the famous Panama City Beach *"strip."* We had an uneventful trip down and settled into our condo.

Eric and his friend were off cruising the strip with plenty of daylight remaining. Everything went great until the last night of the trip. Eric and his friend decided to sneak the car out and go driving along the strip, breaking our agreement. Unfortunately for him, we found out about it and decided to take away his driving privilege for the next three months.

I told him I didn't care if he walked to school or rode the bus. He had made another poor choice, chose his actions, and must live with the consequences. Once again, I had no patience or empathy.

He refused to stay with us when we got home and called his mother to come pick him up. She did not agree with my taking away his driving privilege. He also decided to start living with her full-time instead of each of us half the time. As a result, I made him give his car back to my mother since I decided on the spot that he wouldn't be driving it all in the future.

I should have been thinking to myself and considering the consequences of my actions. But, I was being reactive as I was most often in those days. Remember, I didn't hear Covey's words about *"stimulus and response"* and start my personal leadership journey until 2008, nearly two years after that incident. I was a long way from starting to work on me and was struggling as a parent. But, I thought Eric was the problem.

Knowing and understanding what I know now, I was reacting based on the feelings and values I had at the time. However, my values were not in alignment with natural laws and principles. I valued control, and when I didn't have it, it made me mad, or so I thought.

In ANY situation, between stimulus and response I have the freedom to choose my response.

The stimulus: Eric broke our agreement and took the car out at night. My response: blow up, overreact, blame him, try to control him, act like I own him, and ultimately make him give his car back to my mother.

All of the related thoughts based on my feelings about the situation took me about a second or less to process. There was no pausing between stimulus and response for me at that time in my life. I was an expert at reacting and had no desire to think about my response. My responses came quickly and naturally without any intentional thought. That's who I was and how I operated.

I have grown tremendously since those days. Now, I can see clearly. Nothing made me mad. Eric did not make me mad. I *chose* to be mad.

I chose it all. I chose to get mad and blow up. I could have chosen to stay calm. I chose to blame. I could have chosen to take responsibility my lack of leadership development. I chose to control. I could have chosen to influence. I chose to treat him like an object. I could have chosen to treat him like a person.

Between stimulus and response, I always can and do choose my response. I am responsible.

I made many poor choices. I always let my feelings get in the way. The 2006 incident with Eric's truck was the beginning of four years with very little, if any, influence with Eric. There really wasn't a relationship during those years.

Eric realized he no longer had to be around his reactive dad. He didn't want to be around me anymore and didn't have to be. Therefore, he started making choices that didn't include me or being around me. I had lost all influence with him. This was not my choice, but it was the consequence of my past choices as a parent. When we make our choices, the related consequences automatically come with them.

Stop and Think: If someone overreacts to a situation, are they building trust or creating distrust? Do they have more or less influence than they did before?

Stop and Think: If someone blames you, are they building trust or creating distrust? Do they have more or less influence?

Stop and Think: If someone tries to control you, are they building trust or creating distrust? Do they have more or less influence?

Stop and Think: If someone treats you like an object instead of a person, are they building trust or creating distrust? Do they have more or less influence?

Don't let this happen to you. The issue may not be with your child. It may be with your spouse, a family member, a friend, a neighbor, or a co-worker. If you have already experienced these types of ruptured relationships and want to repair them or prevent this from happening to you in the future, I hope something I share in this book will help you choose to be more proactive.

Luckily, I discovered and started studying the principles of leadership. I became intentional, started improving me, and was able to successfully rebuild and restore my relationship with Eric.

You can always improve too. You are doing it now, as I did when I started making real progress, by reading books written by others wanting to help. I'm still working hard on me and always will be. I read leadership development and personal growth content every day.

I know where the root cause of my problems is. It's in the mirror where it has always been. I can always do something to improve as long as I'm willing to work on the root cause: ME.

Knowing what I know now about being proactive, the first thing I should have done in the situation is *used* the space between stimulus and response to choose my response based on valuing our relationship. After the stimulus, we can choose our response instantly as I did. Or, we can *pause, reflect, and think* before choosing our response as I should have done.

It seems simple now. Back then, this was a foreign

thought. I didn't know there was a space. I didn't understand I really had a choice. To say I was ignorant would be an understatement. I didn't want to know what I didn't know. I thought I already knew it all.

Before I could change what I thought in general and how I thought about stimulus and response, I had to change what I believed.

I believed all of it was Eric's fault. It wasn't. He only had partial responsibility for the situation. But, I had 100% responsibility for me, my actions, and the consequences. I was responsible for not having developed myself as a high impact leader in advance.

I was the parent, the leader, the influencer. Good or bad. Right or wrong. He was the child. I acknowledge his responsibility too, but only for his actions and consequences, not for mine. If I would have been a much better parent from the start, I know he would have been a much better teenager.

"Children need unconditional love more than they need direction." ~ John C. Maxwell

He was 16. I was 37. Ultimately, it was up to me to be responsible. I was the leader. At the time, I was leading at a very low level. Today, I am at a much higher level of leadership. I still make mistakes, but I get it right a lot more often than I did in the past.

I have the responsibility to be sure I blame the right person whenever things go wrong. I am the one to blame. I am responsible. When we think someone else is the problem, that very thought is the problem. Transferring responsibility is the problem. When we think we are responsible, we can become the solution.

A key point to understanding and living a proactive

life is knowing what it means to take responsibility.

For me, taking responsibility required a huge shift as I went from blaming everyone else when things went wrong to looking in the mirror and saying to myself, *"No matter what goes wrong, somehow, someway, I'm responsible for making my situation better. If I value others and want to lead (influence) them positively at a higher level, I'm also responsible for helping make the situation better for them too."*

When we are not valuing others as much as we value ourselves, control, being right, blaming, transferring responsibility, and on and on, we are choosing to be reactive and are operating at a very low level of influence (leadership). We must live with the consequences of our choices. We don't get what we *want* out of life; we get what we *choose* during our life.

High impact leaders take responsibility because they know the impact it has on their influence. Had I paused and asked myself, *"What do I value in this situation?"* with the understanding of natural laws and principles as I understand them today, I would have said, *"I value helping Eric grow and make better decisions while strengthening our relationship."* Then, I would have paused until I came up with a response in alignment with my values.

Stop and Think: When someone wants to help you for your benefit, do they build trust or create distrust? Does their influence increase or decrease?

Be proactive. Take responsibility. How you choose to influence others today determines if you get to influence them in the future. Who we are matters. Why we do what we do matters. Why we say what we say matters.

7

WHO YOU ARE MATTERS

Without Trust, There is No Relationship

*"Be more concerned with your character than your reputation,
because your character is what you really are, while your
reputation is merely what others think you are."*
~ John Wooden

Trust is the foundation of influence (leadership). Our intent is the determining factor in whether we build trust or create distrust. When we attempt to influence others, if they don't feel valued, understand we are seeking mutual benefit, and believe there is a benefit for them, we will not be able to create a foundation of trust to start growing and developing the relationship. They will distrust us and reject our influence.

Stephen R. Covey's son, Stephen M. R. Covey wrote an outstanding book titled *The Speed of Trust*. Without trust, we have no authentic influence. Our influence will be based on how much trust we have built, how strong it is, and how long we have had it.

The Speed of Trust is one of my top five favorite books along with my #1 pick, *The 7 Habits of Highly Effective People*. The other three are by John C. Maxwell: *The 21 Irrefutable Laws of Leadership*, *The 5 Levels of Leadership*, and *The 15 Invaluable Laws of Growth*.

As I grow, change, and continue to read and learn, my top five list seems to always be shifting and changing as well. However, *The 7 Habits of Highly*

Effective People has always remained at the top of my list. I believe it will stay there serving as the foundation for all the rest. If you truly learn and apply what is taught in these five books, you will take your life and your results to an entirely new level.

Numerous studies have revealed, the majority (87%) of our results come from character-based traits (who we are) and only a small amount (13%) of our results come from our competency (what we know). Therefore, we should focus heavily on developing our character.

If you want to truly develop your character and seriously grow and develop your influence, you must self-educate by studying leadership content, identifying leadership principles, and applying leadership principles in all areas of your life, personally and professionally.

Character development matters.

In October 2013 while at the *Blue Ridge Conference on Leadership*, I had the opportunity to hear Colonel Wesley L. Fox, USMC (Retired) speak one evening. As a former member of the USMC, hearing him speak was a special opportunity. He had joined as a Private, served in the Marine Corps 43 years, and is a Medal of Honor recipient. At age 82, he was still making things happen.

Colonel Fox told several stories about different leaders who made an impact on him during his career. He talked about Corporal Myron J. Davis the most. Davis was his squad leader during his first experience in live combat during the Korean War while Colonel Fox was still a Private First Class. Colonel Fox mentioned he trusted Corporal Davis tremendously, as much as any other leader he had during his 43 year career in the USMC. The Colonel shared why his trust in Davis was so strong.

Colonel Fox said, *"We knew he cared for us."*

In those days, the Marines ate their food out of cans. Fox remarked, *"It was so cold everything was frozen including our food. We were demoralized because we had no way of safely warming our food. Therefore, we had to chisel what we wanted to eat from the cans with our bayonets. We only had time to eat at night when we were not in the heat of the battle. In the dark, we could not build fires to keep warm or heat food without exposing our location to the enemy. It's always better to chisel your food from a can in the freezing cold with a bayonet than to be killed eating it with a spoon by a nice, warm fire."*

According to Fox, Corporal Davis realized the impact this was having on the Marines' morale, so he bought them a *"Coleman"* cooking stove to heat their food.

Fox continued, *"Davis always insisted on carrying the stove himself and would never allow another Marine to carry it. He didn't carry it in order to be the first to get to use it because I never saw him use the stove. Davis always passed it straight to the other Marines, and it never made it back to him until it was time to move out. Another thing Davis always did was let the other Marines in his squad pick their meals ahead of him each day. He would always take what was left, which was always corned beef hash."*

Fox said he hoped the Corporal liked it because it was all Davis ever got. With people, little things are big things.

Stop and Think: When someone cares for you, what does it communicate about their intent? Do they build trust or create distrust? Do they have more or less influence?

Colonel Fox closed his remarks by saying, *"There is not one university in the United States offering a four-year degree on leadership. There should be."*

Colonel Fox was still wielding his influence, still serving his country, and still raising up leaders at age 82. I am glad I had the opportunity to meet him. We shook hands a few times, but what I remember most about our interaction before he went on stage was the fist bump he gave me. He was there to do more than communicate. He was also intentionally connecting.

He is a Marine's Marine. A special man. A true hero. Thank you for your service Colonel Fox.

I'm also not aware of a four-year leadership degree from a university. There are plenty of courses offered by colleges and other institutions on leadership. However, if you truly want to develop your leadership potential, the quickest, least expensive, and easiest way to do it is to start reading leadership books and applying what you're learning. You may not receive an official Ph. D. in leadership from a university, but that shouldn't stop you from receiving a Ph. D. in results from society.

As Colonel Fox explained to us, *"Sincerely caring for others is one of the most important building blocks of trust."* It is directly tied to our intent. Most of our influence comes from our character. The more we develop our character, the more useful we become to others. When we intentionally develop our character, we automatically increase our influence with those who are aligned with positive, character-based values.

When it comes to character, remember this. If you fake it, you won't make it. You can see right through someone faking it when it comes to caring for you, others can do the same when it comes to you caring for them. Character is the key. Who you are matters.

DEFINING INFLUENCE

Merriam-Webster's definition of character:
- the way someone thinks, feels, and behaves: someone's personality
- one of the attributes or features that make up and distinguish an individual
- the complex of mental and ethical traits marking and often individualizing a person, group, or nation
- main or essential nature especially as strongly marked and serving to distinguish
- moral excellence and firmness

I define high impact character as: thinking, feeling, and acting in a congruent way while making excellent moral and ethical choices based on self-evident natural laws and principles.

Mahadev Desai, Mahatma Gandhi's secretary, when asked how Gandhi could speak for hours, without notes, while mesmerizing his audiences said, *"What Gandhi thinks, what he feels, what he says, and what he does are all the same. He does not need notes. You and I, we think one thing, feel another, say a third, and do a fourth, so we need notes and files to keep track."*

Desai was describing what it means to be congruent. Gandhi walked the talk. In everything he did, his actions matched his words. He was a real, whole person. His character wasn't fractured.

We need to not only be congruent with what comes out of our mouth, but also what comes out of our heart. We must work constantly to align our words, actions, and beliefs with natural laws and principles. Our ability to live in harmony with these natural laws and principles determines the level of trust we are able to build with others along our leadership journey.

Stop and Think: When someone does what they say they will do or lives how they say they are living, do they build trust or create distrust? Do they have more or less influence if they are congruent? If they are not?

What we think we will do is important. What we say we will do is more important. But, what we actually do is most important. Once we go public with our thoughts, we have made a commitment or promise to be or do something. Now, we either demonstrate congruency, or we don't.

Once we make a commitment to others, we have three options. Although there are three options, there will only be two outcomes. In everything we do, we are either building trust or creating distrust. *Every time, with everyone.*

Three commitment related options:

1) **Build Trust:** Follow through on the commitment and do what we said we would do.
2) **Risk Trust:** Ask to break the commitment and possibly create suspicion of our character.
3) **Create Distrust:** Break the commitment by not doing what we said we would do.

Building Trust

If we are trying to grow our influence with others, we have only one option to get the maximum benefit. We must follow through, keep the commitment, and build trust by making deposits into our trust accounts. Our reputation is on the line. The best time to worry about our reputation is before we have one.

For many, it's too late to maintain trust. They have already created large amounts of distrust. However, if they learn the principles related to building trust, they may be able to restore lost trust. But often, trust is lost forever. Other times, trust is salvageable if they do what they know they should do to make things right.

Stop and Think: When someone makes a commitment to you, do they build trust or create distrust? Does their influence increase or decrease?

Stop and Think: When someone keeps a commitment to you, do they build trust or create distrust? Does their influence increase or decrease?

Risking Trust

This option is tricky and may damage the relationship. Many variables determine if we maintain trust or if we lose trust. Two critical variables to consider are, *"How often do we ask to break a commitment?"* and *"How long has it been since the last time we asked to break a commitment?"*

One reason this option is tricky is because it depends on why we are asking for permission to break the commitment. It depends on how much trust we have already established with the other person. Asking to break a commitment does not automatically make everything okay and result in permission being granted without a cost. Here are several different scenarios to consider before risking trust.

We may ask permission to break the commitment, be denied, and still lose trust simply for asking, although we keep the commitment in the end. Why? We did not value the commitment at the level the other person felt we should. In this case, we had the intent of breaking the commitment although we kept it in the end. Simply asking could create a small amount of distrust or suspicion within the other person.

"In law, a man is guilty when he violates the rights of another. In ethics, he is guilty if he only thinks of doing so."
~ Immanuel Kant

When others start questioning our intent because we are unable or unwilling to keep promises, they will continually grow more suspicious of our character as the number of occurrences increases. The time between occurrences will always be a consideration too.

Stop and Think: Generally speaking, if someone expresses their intent to break a commitment with you, are they building trust or creating distrust? Is their influence with you more likely to increase or decrease?

Another scenario related to *risking trust* could be asking permission to break a commitment and receiving permission but still losing some trust in the end. We may earn trust for asking permission to break the promise. However, since we didn't follow through with our original commitment, we may lose more trust than we gained. Therefore, the total trust transaction ends up being a negative. Although we are released from the commitment, we may still be creating distrust.

"The moment there is suspicion about a person's motives, everything he does becomes tainted." ~ Mahatma Gandhi

Stop and Think: Generally speaking, when someone asks to break a promise or commitment with you after you have already made plans and you choose to release them from the commitment, how much does their asking to be released from the commitment affect your trust in them going forward? How does it affect their influence if they do it often?

Let's consider asking permission to break a promise, but not receiving permission. They hold us to it. However, we break the commitment any way. We not only create distrust for breaking the initial promise, but we also create additional distrust for giving them the false impression they actually had influence in the situation. By asking their permission to break the commitment, and then, ignoring their answer, we create additional distrust.

In this scenario, if we know that no matter what the person says we are going to break the commitment, we would be better off to tell them we are going to break the promise up front and create distrust once instead of hoping to be released from the promise and creating more distrust when we are not but choose to break the commitment anyway.

Stop and Think: If someone made a promise to you and they ask you to release them from it, but you don't, and they break the promise anyway, do they create more distrust than if they would have simply broken the promise without consulting you? Would they have more or less influence with you if they chose to be open and honest with you from the start?

Creating Distrust

If you don't do what you say you will do or be who you say you will be, you will create distrust. When we intentionally or unintentionally break a promise, we are creating significant distrust. It's easy to do. If we are not careful, we can make it much more complicated than it needs to be.

If we make excuses, we are adding to the total amount of distrust. If we lie about it, we are making it worse. If we are going to create distrust intentionally, we should go ahead and live up to it. At least, we have the chance of earning a slight bit of trust for taking responsibility and being honest. Overall, there will still be distrust because we are making a withdrawal from the trust account.

Stop and Think: If someone breaks a promise with you, do they build trust or create more distrust by making excuses or lying about it? Do you feel they have more integrity if they own up to it? Does their influence increase or decrease if they make excuses? Does their influence increase or decrease if they lie?

Making and keeping commitments is between you and you. When you make commitments, don't make them lightly. Making commitments is important. When you make them, you create hope. When you keep them, you build trust. When you break them, you create distrust.

8

CHARACTER COUNTS

Our Character Makes Us or Breaks Us

"Good character is more to be praised than outstanding talent.
Most talents are, to some extent, a gift.
Good character, by contrast, is not given to us.
We have to build it piece by piece: by thought, choice,
courage, and determination." ~ John Luther

Henry Cloud, author of *integrity*, defines character as, *"the ability to meet the demands of reality."*

While reading *integrity*, I developed an understanding of Cloud's perspective which led me to further develop my understanding of what character is and the impact it has on all we do.

No matter what we are faced with in life such as, hardships, struggles, losses, setbacks, challenges, failures, and defeat, if we cannot handle it effectively, it is due to a flaw in our character. Somewhere within our character we need improvement and growth. Weakness of character is causing us to be ineffective. We must find the weakness and develop it into an asset instead of a liability.

Think back to the stories I've shared about Eric, when I took his truck and eventually his car away from him. Why did I deal with the situation ineffectively? I had many character flaws.

We all have blind spots and must depend on others we trust to help us identify them. I still have plenty of opportunity, but I have improved a lot since those days.

My biggest character flaw relative to both of those situations was my lack of patience. When we are exhibiting impatience, we are showing the world a flaw in our character.

Merriam-Webster's definition of patience:
- able to remain calm and not become annoyed when waiting for a long time or when dealing with problems or difficult people
- done in a careful way over a long period of time without hurrying

When we cannot deal effectively with the speed something is happening or the fact we cannot get what we want, we are suffering from a character flaw.

Think of the child throwing a temper tantrum when they don't get what they want. It makes them mad, so they do the only thing they can to try to get their way. They try to annoy us into submission with their screams and erratic behavior. Sometimes, they get their way. Sometimes, they don't. It's easy to see they cannot control themselves. Often, neither can we.

Lack of patience leads to lack of control.

In the story about Eric, I valued controlling him. I had much work to do on me. I had no thoughts of growth and development. I didn't realize I was not being a good leadership example. Developing and controlling are character traits. Developing others is positive and in alignment with natural laws and principles. Controlling others is negative and not in alignment with natural laws and principles.

We choose our values. Our values influence our thoughts which influence our feelings which influence our actions. Choices convert our values into action.

Our choices based on our values reveal our character to others. Good choices reveal good character. Bad choices reveal bad character. Good character says easy, but it does hard until you have made it a habit and changed who you are at the very core.

Stop and Think: Which character traits should a person possess in order to build more trust? Which character traits would allow a person to have more influence?

"Your character growth determines the height of your personal growth. Without personal growth, you can never reach your potential." ~ John C. Maxwell

Reflecting on John's words, I think about the many people I have met in my career stuck on the bottom of the *"corporate ladder"* with tremendous potential.

These people have more competency than character. They have tons of potential held back by a dam constructed of poor character. They are very sharp, very capable, and could potentially be in a higher position with better pay, more responsibility, and more influence. Unfortunately, many believe the world is out to get them. They feel they cannot catch a break. The real problem is they are not willing to accept responsibility for developing themselves.

If you have seen the movie *The Sixth Sense* with Bruce Willis, you will remember the kid saying he sees dead people. I often see *"confused"* people. They think it's the world's fault they are where they are, but in reality it's no one's fault but their own. They are responsible for the choices they make which either develops or destroys their character. Ultimately, their character is holding them back. We can destroy our character quickly, but we can't build it quickly. Character building takes time and discipline.

You will know when you encounter a *"confused"* person. They may be telling you how *"the man"* is out to get them. Or, how their co-workers are against them. Or, how they work much harder than others but continuously get passed up for promotions or pay increases. Or, they know how to do all the jobs but get overlooked for promotions. They focus on blame.

They are not necessarily bad people with bad intentions. They are simply confused about who is responsible for their lives. They have character work to do because they are unable to meet the demands of reality. We all have more work to do because we all want more out of life.

They usually perform their tasks very well but remain at the bottom of the ladder. When you meet someone and they are on the bottom of the ladder with years of experience and don't want to be there, there is a reason they are there. The reason is their character flaws are holding them back.

This scenario doesn't apply to a young person starting out or someone changing careers. It's related to someone sharp and seemingly out of place. Someone appearing to have much more to offer. They do, but they have not overcome their character flaws to release their true potential.

Remember the words from John Maxwell, *"We get hired for what we know, but we get fired for who we are."* I bet you have seen this play out in your career. I'm sure you already know that not everyone who should be fired gets fired. Unfortunately, some hang on because they work hard and can produce. Their competency allows them to hang on to the ladder, but their character keeps them from climbing it.

Undoubtedly, they get hired for what they know, but many of them do not make it past the level for which they are hired. They remain stuck in *"ladder lock."* They are not climbing because of *who they are*. It does not matter where they are on the ladder. If their competency is higher than their position, their character is holding them back.

Many take the easy way out and continue to develop their competency in an attempt to fix everything. They go back to college. They take another course. They get another degree. These things are great but make a minimal impact without the support of good, solid character.

What good will three degrees do us if we cannot get along with people? Not much good. We may not be able to get a job or keep a job. To be effective in this world, we must be able to work with others. To be highly effective, we must be able to work through others.

If we do become more educated, we may be smarter and know more than others. But if we cannot get along with people, nothing much will change. If we do not work on our character, we will not be much better off in our professional career, no matter how much we educate ourselves.

Sometimes, character and competency level off at the same time. This is called the *Peter Principle* which states, *"People get promoted to their level of incompetency, and there they remain."* It's not only about competency, but also character.

When this happens, people do not want to take a hard look in the mirror and do the character work necessary to continue to develop the needed competency to excel. Their competency may have gotten them the position, but it may not be enough to meet the requirements of the position. They must grow by learning more and doing more to excel.

Their character flaws are preventing them from applying themselves. They need to develop additional competencies in order to be effective. Instead of choosing to grow, they choose to coast. This isn't good for them or those around them.

"Ninety-nine percent of leadership failures are failures in character." ~ Norman Schwarzkopf

People with a high degree of character develop the necessary competency needed to get to where they want to go. They have the ability to meet the demands of reality. With strong character, they find a way to make it happen.

Unfortunately, many people with a high degree of competency never develop the character required to get them to where they want to go. They have a blind spot and cannot see their problem in the mirror.

One reason is that many of these people already think they are smarter than almost everyone else. Let's assume they are correct. They are smarter than most of the others around them doing similar jobs or jobs they want to be doing. This means they place a high value on intellectual knowledge which is great. Being smarter than others is not a problem. Thinking and acting like we are smarter than others is a problem. It's a character flaw and may lead to isolation and limitation where our influence is decreased.

Knowledge alone is not enough. It's not the smartest

who will win the battle although there may be a place for them on the field. No one should be on the field unless they add to the effectiveness of the team by connecting and cooperating in a synergistic manner. We need to reflect back to Henry Cloud's definition of character, *"the ability to meet the demands of reality."* In this case, teamwork is a demand of reality. Some people have not developed the ability to work well with a team. They could, but they haven't. Until they do, they will remain stuck.

> *"The significant problems we face cannot be solved at the same level of thinking we were at when we created them."*
> ~ *Albert Einstein*

If we are having trouble with people, it is a character issue. Our character issue. The solution does not lie within them. It lies within us. We are the problem and the solution, but only if we choose to start looking in the mirror.

The amazing thing is our problem with people has absolutely nothing to do with them and everything to do with us. We must fully understand; we are the problem.

If we think our problems are someone else's fault, we are in denial. If they never change, our problems will never change. Until we accept responsibility, we are leaving a lot of potential influence on the table. We are leaving much success on the table. We are leaving many wins on the table. If we find ourselves blaming others, we must ask, *"How can I take responsibility and proactively resolve the issue?"*

Since asking myself the same question, I have been working on me and continue to work on me. Things are better and are always getting better as a result. The majority of my work happens in the mirror.

Before learning what I'm sharing with you, I had a tremendous amount of character work to do. I was young and thought I had the world figured out, while fully believing nearly everyone else was the problem.

While growing and learning, I've realized I don't get closer to knowing it all every time I read a book. I actually get farther away from knowing it all because I become more aware of all there is to learn.

Imagine your knowledge, what you know. It's represented as the surface area of a dime lying flat. The outside edge, perimeter of the dime, represents your awareness of what you don't know, your *perimeter of awareness*. You're also unaware of all the knowledge beyond your perimeter of awareness that's found in your *area of ignorance*. You start growing and increase your knowledge from the size of a dime to the size of a dinner plate. Your knowledge has increased and is much more impressive indeed.

As your knowledge increased, what happened to your awareness relative to what you didn't know, your perimeter of awareness? It always increases as your knowledge increases.

The more you know, the more you realize what you don't know. I often call this *"dumber by the book."* I thought I only got smarter by reading books. I have increased my actual knowledge. But, relative to my awareness of what I don't know, a funny thing happens. I feel less knowledgeable and become more aware of my ignorance.

I am learning more while at the same time learning there is more to be learned. Using this illustration, those thinking they know it all really don't know much. They have a very small perimeter of awareness.

I realize there are many people blaming others as I did in the past. They don't know what they don't know because their area of knowledge is small. It will be hard for them to accept this concept and take action. It will not happen overnight, but it will happen if they commit to personal growth and the application of leadership principles.

I didn't know what I didn't know. I was blaming others for my circumstances and for holding me back. I could easily find a reason to avoid responsibility and blame others.

What did they have to do with me? I thought what they were doing had everything to do with me. Today, I understand what they were doing had NOTHING to do with me. I thought my problem was with them. It wasn't. My problem was me.

"Self-mastery is the hardest job you'll ever tackle. If you do not conquer self, you will be conquered by self. You may see at one and the same time both your best friend and your greatest enemy, by stepping in front of a mirror." ~ Napoleon Hill

Speaking of seeing your worst enemy in the mirror, I realize the enemy is me, now and in my past. We can change for the better whenever we're ready. We must take responsibility for ourselves and stop placing our livelihood in the hands of others who don't care if we succeed or fail.

The world will change for us, when we change for the world.

As high impact leaders, regardless of the situation, we look in the mirror and take the blame when things are going wrong. When we do, we demonstrate the high level character trait of taking responsibility. Likewise, when things are going right as high impact leaders, we look through the window and give others the credit. When we do, we are demonstrating the high level character trait of humility.

Stop and Think: Who do you trust more, someone blaming others when things go wrong or someone taking the blame when things go wrong? Which one would have more influence?

Stop and Think: Who do you trust more, someone taking the credit when things go right or someone giving credit to others when things go right? Which one would have more influence?

"Character is a quality that embodies many important traits such as integrity, courage, perseverance, confidence, and wisdom. Unlike your fingerprints that you were born with and cannot change, character is something that you create within yourself and must take responsibility for changing." ~ Jim Rohn

9

CHARACTER IS DEVELOPED DAILY, NOT IN A DAY

To Develop Our Character, We Must Begin Within

"What lies behind us and what lies ahead of us are tiny matters compared to what lives within us." ~ Henry David Thoreau

Trust happens on the outside, but it starts on the inside.

We cannot make people trust us no matter how hard we try. If we want to establish trust with others, we must *begin within*. We must make trustworthy choices. Then, others can make the choice to trust or distrust us based on who they believe we are.

The character traits we choose to value and internalize ultimately determine our level of influence. We must exhibit the right behavior for the right traits at the right time for the right reason in order to be seen as trustworthy. If we slip just once, we will foster suspicion. We will stir the subconscious *"trust"* radar in others. They will be on full alert.

We are constantly scanning and evaluating the trustworthiness of those around us, keeping tally consciously and subconsciously of the distrust being created and the trust being built. We know who we can and cannot trust.

We lose trust much more quickly than we build it.

Trust and distrust are valued differently depending on what the individual sees, feels, and believes. Your goal should be to focus on intentionally using your knowledge and influence to choose to make every effort to connect with and build trust with others. You must also know you will create automatic distrust without knowing it if you are around someone long enough and often enough.

How can you strengthen your character? Where should you start? The answer is different for everyone. We are all unique. But, when it comes to character, we must always begin within.

With character, you always want to focus on your areas of weakness. This is where you have the greatest opportunity for improvement. Relative to competency, always focus on your strengths where you are naturally good and can become exceptional.

Character is the foundation of relationships. Therefore, it is the key to influence. No one can choose what area of character you need to focus on but you. Likewise, no one can work on strengthening your character but you. This is an issue between you and you.

You should have already been thinking deeply and reflecting on your character. Character traits have a big impact on your influence. They all matter. You may need to do additional research to find information on the specific traits you want to learn more about.

There are many, many character traits. I want to focus on five that I consider critical: integrity, courage, perseverance, confidence, and humility.

INTEGRITY

Merriam-Webster's definition of integrity:
- the quality of being honest and fair
- the state of being complete or whole

DEFINING INFLUENCE

*"The greatest way to live in honor in this world is to be what
we pretend to be. To be in reality what we want
others to think we are." ~ Socrates*

Integrity is the trait most people reference when
asked, *"What is trust?"* What they actually say is honesty
which is one of several components of integrity.
Integrity is very important, but it is only one of the
many character traits forming your unique character.

To illustrate the strength of each individual trait,
assume you meet someone and everything you know
about their character is outstanding. It could not be
better. You absolutely trust them. Then, you discover
they have told you a lie. What happened to their
trustworthiness and your trust in them? You lost some
amount of trust in them because of one revealed
character flaw. You will also become more suspicious
of them in the future.

To be dishonest or honest is a choice. The more
integrity someone has the less they lie. The less integrity
they have the more they lie. Many different character
traits come into play when choosing to lie or tell the
truth. Courage or lack of courage is often behind the
choice of whether to lie or tell the truth.

Stop and Think: When you have been dishonest with
others in the past, what character traits were you weak
in? What do you need to do to strengthen them?

*"None of us can keep another from having a bad opinion of us,
but we can make sure it isn't true." ~ John Weston*

People are going to say things, maybe bad things.
They always have. They always will. However, we

determine if what they say is true or not. No one else can decide who we are. We decide who we are. Our actions, not someone else's opinion, determine if we are truly trustworthy.

Stop and Think: When you have been honest with others in situations where you considered being dishonest, what character traits did you rely on to keep you honest?

Merriam-Webster's definition of lying:
-   creating a false or misleading impression

One of the little things that's a big thing with many people and is a red flag when evaluating someone's character is: Will they be on time for meetings or appointments? Will they be late? If they are late, do they care?

Some people don't seem to realize *"late"* is a synonym for *"lie."* When we are late, we are demonstrating to others we do not value their time. Imagine being late and walking into a meeting with someone or a group of people we want to positively influence and saying, *"I am late because I don't value your time."* What would happen to our influence?

When we're late, we may not be saying it with our words, but we are definitely saying it with our actions. It does sound a little better when we show up sincerely saying, *"I am sorry for being late."* Is it a rare occasion when we are late, or is it a normal occurrence? I have not heard anyone show up late saying, *"Sorry, I lied to everyone. I hope you don't mind."* Many people do not think twice about being late. They think it's okay to lie to someone and call it something different, expecting the play on words to somehow justify their actions.

If everyone else does something, it doesn't mean it's the right thing to do. Lead your own life. Do what you say you will do when you say you will do it because it's the right thing to do.

"In matters of fashion, swim with the current. In matters of conscience, stand like a rock." ~ Thomas Jefferson

No matter what we call it, when we schedule an appointment with someone and are late, or worse do not show up at all, we have made a false or misleading impression. We said we would do something, and we didn't. What we call it does not change the impact on trust and influence.

Stop and Think: When you have arranged your schedule to meet with someone and they do not show up on time, do they build trust or create distrust? Does their influence with you increase or decrease? What if they don't show up at all?

Each character trait impacts trust. You can play out this scenario with every character trait being *"the one in question."* The result will be the same: lost trust, suspicion, and decreased influence. Your integrity is important and is made up of more components than honesty alone.

Fairness is a component of integrity. How do you know when someone treats you fairly or unfairly? No one taught you the thousands of ways you could be treated unfairly. Without question, you feel it when it happens.

Fairness is about feeling. If you feel you were treated

fairly in a situation, in your mind, you were. If you feel you were treated unfairly, although you were not, the effect on trust is the same as if you were. You can lose trust with people based on their perception. The old saying, *"perception is reality"* definitely applies here. Fairness is rooted in feelings when we believe we have been or are being treated unequally.

"There is nothing so unequal as the equal treatment of unequals."
~ Ken Blanchard

Stop and Think: When you feel someone has treated you unfairly, do they build trust or create distrust? Does their influence increase or decrease?

In Henry Cloud's book *integrity*, he defines integrity as, *"the courage to meet the demands of reality."* Remember, he also defined character as, *"the ability to meet the demands of reality."* Courage is heavily weighted in the character equation. There is a huge difference in having the ability to do something and having the courage to actually do it.

"When I was a kid, one of my father's favorite riddles to us went like this:
'Five frogs are sitting on a log. Four decide to jump off.
How many are left?'
The first time he asked me I answered one.
'No,' he responded. 'Five.
Why? Because there's a difference between deciding and doing!'"
~ John C. Maxwell

Often, the difference between deciding and doing is courage.

COURAGE

Merriam-Webster's definition of courage:
- the ability to do something you know is difficult or dangerous

"Only those who will risk going too far can possibly find out how far one can go." ~ T. S. Eliot

Courage has a significant impact on your character and your life. Knowing the right thing to do and doing the right thing is not the same thing. There is a big gap between knowing and doing. Often, the only bridge connecting the two is courage. You must cross it in order to build your character and to do what's right.

In order to do whatever you perceive as difficult, dangerous, risky, or uncomfortable, you must overcome something within you. Only you know what that is. Only you can make the changes necessary to take action. Making those changes takes courage.

When you exhibit courage, you may feel afraid. You can be courageous and fearful at the same time. I am sure you have done things in your life and were afraid while you were doing them. Courage is about taking action in the face of fear.

"I learned that courage was not the absence of fear, but the triumph over it. The brave man is not he who does not feel afraid, but he who conquers that fear."
~ Nelson Mandela

All of our growth happens outside of our comfort zone. Courage allows us to move beyond our comfort zone. If we are in our comfort zone, we are not growing. That's why we are comfortable.

Courage allows you to transform yourself from who you are today to who you want to become tomorrow. Courage allows you to look at your circumstances no matter how difficult they may be and say to yourself, "*I have a choice. I can change my circumstances. I will do it no matter the adversity I may face.*"

Whenever I think of courage, I think of Ria. She became a John Maxwell Certified Coach, Trainer, and Speaker in February 2013 and quickly made a goal to leave her position as the Director of Regulatory Affairs and Compliance at our local hospital within one year. She had spent her entire career earning degrees and certifications to grow and advance in the medical field. She resigned her corporate job on January 3, 2014 to pursue her dream to become an author, professional leadership coach, trainer, and keynote speaker.

It did not take much courage to make the decision to leave her comfort zone. However, it did take tremendous courage to actually do it. Remember John's story about the five frogs sitting on the log and the difference between deciding and doing? She did more than decide to do it. She took action and did it.

I share the following with her permission. Ria is a model of courage. She has exhibited courage continuously since I first met her. At the time, she was 19 and living in circumstances most of us cannot imagine. I had no idea until several months later when there was enough trust for her to reveal she was being sexually abused by her father, the person that should have been protecting her the most. It had started when she was 12 years old and continued until she told me.

You would have never known it. Once I became aware of it, it took courage on my part to help her escape the situation. But, it took much more courage for her to choose to escape the situation while leaving her family and the only life she had known behind.

I am proud of the person she has revealed to the world. This is who she has been all along. She has never let her past circumstances, which as a child were beyond her control, hold her back for one minute. She is writing her autobiography, *Ria's Story from Ashes to Beauty*, and plans to share *her* story with the world to give hope and inspiration to others who are or have faced adversity. She is a *Courage Warrior!* You can learn more about Ria, her story, and her many books at RiaStory.com.

She has already started traveling around the country to share her story and help others realize they are not what happened to them. She recently shared her story on stage at a Les Brown event in Los Angeles, California. She is a courageous woman.

Think of something bad that happens to people every day such as: accidents, abuse, crime, disease, loss, war, etc. Imagine this happening to three different people. Consider the following three scenarios:

1) Imagine one person not being able to deal with it, shutting off from the world, turning to drugs and alcohol, or taking their own life.

2) Imagine the second person dealing effectively with it and living life like it never happened.

3) Imagine the third person, in an effort to help prevent others from allowing the bad experience to ruin their lives, writing a book and speaking publicly about it to give others hope and to let them know they can move past what happened to them and lead a happy, healthy, and productive life.

This is a realistic scenario likely playing out every day. What is the difference in these three people? Why was there three different outcomes?

Imagine there was no difference in what happened to them. But, there was a difference in their response to what happened to them. Each made different choices afterward. There was a difference in the amount of integrity, courage, perseverance, confidence, and humility each chose to bring forth.

The difference was their character: the ability to meet the demands of reality. And, their integrity: the courage to meet the demands of reality.

What's most important is not what happens to us, but our response to what happens to us. We cannot always control what happens to us. But, we can control our response to what happens to us which means we can influence much, but not all, of what happens to us in the future.

Stop and Think: Does your response in any situation influence much of what happens to you in the future?

Stop and Think: Are you exactly where you should be today based on all of your responses (choices) leading up today? If you think you should be somewhere else based on your choices, why are you not there? Why are you instead where you are? Isn't it because of your choices?

You have the freedom to choose your response in any situation. However, you often need courage in order to make the choice, but the choice is always yours. Your choices shape you, your life, and the lives of others. Courage is a choice too. For many, it is a difficult choice, but it is a choice anyone can make.

For some, courage can be the difference between life and death. Many people have perished because they could not muster up the courage to face the situation they were in, be proactive, and take responsibility for changing their circumstances. There are many examples throughout history where courage has led people out of dire, unimaginable circumstances leaving the rest of us asking, *"How did they do it?"*

PERSEVERANCE

Merriam-Webster's definition of perseverance:
-   the continued effort to do or achieve something despite difficulties, failure, or opposition

"Never, never, never give up!" ~ *Winston Churchill*

Perseverance is about, never giving up. No matter how hard it is. No matter how long it takes. No matter how many people say you cannot do it. No matter how many people tell you it's impossible. No matter how many people say you will fail. No matter how much opposition there is against it. If you want to do something, you must NEVER GIVE UP!

Stop and Think: Who do you trust more to come through for you, someone willing to stick with it until they accomplish the task or someone willing to give up when it gets hard? Which person has more influence?

Consider for a moment the things you have accomplished in your life because you never gave up. You should feel great knowing you kept fighting for what you wanted. Now, think of the things you started but failed to finish. For some reason, you simply gave up at some point. This feeling is probably not so good.

What would be different today if you would not have given up but instead persevered until you reached the goal? What inside of you caused you to give up? Remember the choice formula: What you think + What you feel + What you do = Choice.

How we think determines when or if we give up. It determines if we never give up. This is why we must change the way we think. If we want to do something or achieve something we never have, we must think in a way we never have. We must become someone we have never been. The way we think is the key to accomplishing everything in life we want to achieve personally and professionally.

We must do more than want what we want. We must become what we want to be. We must do more than think differently. We must actually be different.

Do you want to persevere and be around and associate with others who don't give up?

If so, you must demonstrate perseverance. As with most leadership principles, it says easy and does hard. When you demonstrate never giving up, you attract people with perseverance. You don't see people with perseverance associating regularly with people who quit when the going gets tough.

One of the major obstacles to perseverance is the fear of failure. Many people become worried about what others say and think as they struggle to persevere and never give up. Remember our last trait: courage. Can you see how the traits tie together? It is not about one character trait. It's about all of them.

Those offering you criticism and ridiculing you,

when you don't give up, do not have a high degree of perseverance themselves. They do not understand. They cannot understand. Their level of awareness relative to perseverance is much lower than yours.

If you can't take it, you won't make it. You will quit. DO NOT QUIT! You *can* take it. It's a choice that only you can make.

"A hero is no braver than an ordinary man, but he is brave five minutes longer." ~ Ralph Waldo Emerson

The hero often is the hero only because he or she exhibited greater perseverance than those they were among.

To illustrate perseverance, consider how we learn to walk. Without perseverance, we would never walk.

Who taught you how to walk? Many believe it was their parents. Did your parents teach you balance and coordination? Or, did you teach yourself? They didn't teach us. They only supported us by holding our hands, putting us in a walker, or giving us endless encouragement. Imagine if they had done the opposite and held us back or tried to prevent us from walking because they were afraid we might get hurt.

We taught ourselves to walk didn't we? At the time we learned to walk, most of us could not speak or truly understand any language. Which character trait, that you've had inside since birth, did you start to develop and bring forth as a toddler that ultimately allowed you to teach yourself how to walk? It was perseverance.

The key to perseverance is having the burning desire to never give up. For example, any baby physically capable of walking will walk. Babies do not give up. They persevere until they accomplish the task.

They do not care how many times they fall down. They do not care if they get hurt. They do not care if people laugh while they are learning. They are oblivious to everything but their burning desire to walk. They never give up!

How do they do it? They do not allow outside influence, circumstances, or past failures to determine their outcome. They simply never stop trying to achieve the goal. They choose to determine the outcome.

We were all born with perseverance. This is only one example, but many character traits allowed us to grow and develop into a functioning human being. What happens to the burning desire to never give up within us all? Who extinguishes the flame? It's you. You are the only person who can extinguish the flame burning within. No one else can extinguish your flame unless you give them permission.

We often blame others when we quit. But, quitting is our choice which means we must take responsibility. We must admit, *"I quit. I gave up."* Most of us don't want the responsibility, so we blame others, the circumstances, the environment, the government, and on and on and on. We are responsible for our choices.

We all allow others to begin to influence us as we grow and develop. However, we must fully understand they do not *determine* our choices. They only *influence* them. We always have the space between stimulus and response to choose our response.

"The first step toward success is taken when you refuse to be a captive of the environment in which you first find yourself."
~ Mark Caine

We make our first mistake when we start to accept

negative influence from others. Others believing there is no way they can do it, so there must be no way we can do it. Others who have failed, so they think we will fail. Others who think it's not worth it to them, so it must not be worth it to us. Others who are not succeeding in their life and don't want to see us succeeding in our life. Others who quit when it gets hard, and think we will quit when it gets hard.

Break the pattern. Do not accept negative influence. Do not let people influence you if they are not already getting the results you desire. It's your choice. It will always be your choice. Are you consciously exercising your freedom to choose which influence you will accept and which influence you will reject?

Stop and Think: When you see people being negatively influenced by others, do you trust their ability to lead themselves well? Do they have more or less influence?

Stephen R. Covey describes this as the *"social mirror"* surrounding us all. As a child when you begin to grow older, learn to speak, learn to understand a language, and begin to interact with more people, you became much more susceptible to the influence of others; and you started exchanging thoughts with others. The rest of the world does not necessarily think like you think.

This can be a very positive thing with a tremendous impact on your life for the better as you synergize with others. Or, it can be a very negative thing with devastating results on your life. There are examples where people have worked together to accomplish great things. There are also examples where someone started hanging around the wrong crowd and ultimately went in to a state of decline.

As you continue your journey to grow and develop your influence (leadership), you must persevere. Never give up on continuing to grow and to develop your character traits. Be sure to give special attention to those in which you are weak. Those are the ones holding you back. They are preventing you from having the influence you desire. Who you are matters. What you do matters. How you do it matters.

NEVER, NEVER, NEVER, GIVE UP!

"Life is not easy for any of us. But what of that? We must have perseverance and above all confidence in ourselves. We must believe that we are gifted for something and that this thing must be attained." ~ Marie Curie

CONFIDENCE

Merriam-Webster's definition of confidence:
- a feeling or belief you can do something well or succeed at something
- a feeling or belief someone or something is good or has the ability to succeed at something
- the feeling of being certain something will happen or something is true

"Believe in yourself! Have faith in your abilities! Without a humble but reasonable confidence in your powers, you cannot be successful or happy." ~ Norman Vincent Peale

No matter how much someone else believes in you, you must believe in yourself. You can borrow belief from others to get going, but to be highly effective, you ultimately must believe in yourself.

Stop and Think: Who do you trust more, someone with confidence or someone without confidence? Which type of person has more influence?

If you have a lot of confidence, great. If you don't, how do you get it? You must stop associating with others who don't have confidence in themselves or you. You must start building relationships with those who do have confidence in themselves and in you.

This is especially true when you are struggling to gain confidence. In order to gain confidence, you must start having small victories, small wins. The first small victory you need to have is knowing someone else has confidence in you although you may not have it in yourself.

Has anyone ever believed in you when you didn't believe in yourself? Did they give you confidence? Did they pick you up? Did you trust them more? Did you get closer to them? Did you enjoy being around them?

They were lifting you up. They were loaning you their confidence until you could develop it inside of yourself. These people are special. They care about us. They want to help us. And, they are rare.

These people are out there for us. If you need them, take responsibility and seek them out. When you find them, you need to do all you can to develop a strong, positive relationship with them. You must also realize, you can be this special person for someone else. Lifting others always lifts you.

Stop and Think: If someone has confidence in you, do you trust them more or less? Do they have more or less influence?

You may not know anyone able or willing to help lift you up. You are not out of luck. We can motivate ourselves. We can get inside the greatest minds by simply reading the books they have written. Stimulating your mind helps motivate, inspire, and grow you.

I read, read, and then read some more. The majority of my external motivation comes from people I've never met, but they still impacted me and shaped my life. Reading increases my confidence and is a daily habit that I will never abandon.

This very topic is one of the motivating factors for me. I want to lift people I may never meet as many of the authors I have never met have lifted me. I want to make a positive difference in the lives of others. I want to loan you my confidence. You have much to offer and can make a greater impact in the lives of others.

There is hope. You can do what you want to do. There should be no doubt in your mind. You can take yourself to the next level. Then, start over and do it again and again.

Your potential is infinite. As long as you are alive, you can get better. It's a matter of choice. Will you develop the potential within you? You're doing it right now. You are reading and growing. You know what I know. We can always get better if we simply make the right choices.

Many times when we want to improve, we often try to figure out what we should start doing which is great. No doubt, we definitely need to start doing things differently if we want to get different results. However, we can get different results if we choose to stop doing certain things too. Sometimes, it may be more difficult to *stop* doing something old than to *start* doing something new.

Two of the best things I've done was to stop doing things leading me in the wrong direction or wasting my time, money, and energy. I stopped blaming anyone and anything outside of myself for my circumstances. I stopped consuming alcohol. Both were wasting my time and keeping me from reaching my potential.

Make a list of things you need to stop doing. Put this list somewhere you will see it every day. Commit to read it every day. Add notes related to the benefits you will gain if you stop doing these things. Reflect often on the positive changes that await you.

If we are not making something happen, we are waiting for something to happen. Do you think there is a difference in our confidence if we stop waiting for something to happen and start making things happen?

Leading yourself well boosts your confidence. Small wins always lead to big wins.

"If it's to be, it's up to me." ~ Truett Cathy

Stop and Think: What do you need to stop doing to create a positive change in your life? What is the one thing holding you back the most?

Stop and Think: If you know someone wants to stop doing something and they have the self-control to do it, do they build trust or create distrust? Do they have more or less influence?

Stop and Think: Do you trust those leading themselves well more or less than those who are not? Which type of person has the most influence?

"We become the combined average of the five people we hang around the most. We start to eat what they eat, drink what they drink, talk like they talk, read what they read, think like they think, watch what they watch, and dress like they dress."
~ *Jim Rohn*

Rohn's words ring true. We also start to get the results they get.

You will begin to outgrow others as you increase your confidence. As you do, you must make tough decisions.

You must begin to transition away from people who are not supportive of you and your goals. Those unable to express high confidence in themselves and you will never be able to help and support you. They will lean on you. You do not need people to lean on you and hold you in place. You need people to lift you to a higher place.

Stop and Think: Do you trust people more or less based on their choice of friends? Does their influence increase or decrease because of their associations?

When you begin to grow, be ready for the comments from the *"anchor draggers"* in your life. They want to hold you back. They will make comments like this:

- *Are you sure about this?*
- *I'm not sure if you'll be able to do it.*
- *Do you know how hard it's going to be?*
- *I hope you don't end up wasting your time.*
- *You better think about what you're about to do.*
- *I wouldn't do that if I were you.*

You will hear similar comments as you start building your confidence and doing new things. The comments will decrease as people decide to grow with you or go away from you.

Whatever you are doing, you can always do more. The real question is, *"Are you willing to do more?"* You must first believe in yourself. Then, you must develop yourself. Lastly, you must bet on yourself. Do these three things, and you will make something happen you have never made happen in the past.

> *"If you are trying to achieve, there will be roadblocks. I've had them; everybody has had them. But obstacles don't have to stop you. If you run into a wall, don't turn around and give up. Figure out how to climb it, go through it, or work around it."*
> *~ Michael Jordan*

Every door is a wall until you go through it. Life is full of walls. You must have the confidence to do as Jordan said, *"Figure out how to climb it, go through it, or work around it."* Rest assured, once you get past one wall, there will be another one in your path. That's life. If you are living, you will encounter walls. You decide whether or not they stop you. If you're not running into walls, you're not going anywhere.

As you continue to grow and build your confidence, you must realize one thing, you will not always win. Sometimes, you will lose. I will lose. We all lose eventually. It is inevitable. It happens. We will make mistakes and experience loss as we grow.

> *"The good times we put in our pocket.*
> *The bad times we put in our heart."* ~ *Les Brown*

If we are learning while we're losing, we really aren't losing. Learning is never losing. Learning is preparing to win.

Humility allows us to learn from our mistakes. It's about our perspective. We must set ourselves up for small wins and be consistent if we want to increase our confidence.

Stop and Think: When people learn from their mistakes, do they build trust or create distrust relative to their ability to deal with adversity? What does this reveal about their character? Does their influence increase or decrease?

Stop and Think: When people make the same mistake over and over without learning, do they build trust or create distrust? What does this reveal about their character? Does their influence increase or decrease?

HUMILITY

Merriam-Webster's definition of humility:
- the quality or state of not thinking you are better than other people

"Humility is not thinking less of yourself,
it's thinking of yourself less." ~ C. S. Lewis

Relative to humility, we should add value to ourselves but not focus on ourselves. We should value our achievements and successes, but we should focus on helping others achieve and succeed. Humility is a hard character trait to develop for some. However, humility will strengthen the other character traits.

As you grow and get results, who you become during the process will greatly impact your influence. You can be very confident and be humble at the same time. The key is how you are *being* while you are confident. Humility is the foundation for confidence while pride and ego make up the foundation for conceit.

Merriam-Webster's definition of conceit:
- too much pride in your own worth or goodness

Merriam-Webster's definition of conceited:
- having or showing an excessively high opinion of oneself

Confidence and conceit are separated by a very fine line. The instant the positive confidence we have on the inside is expressed with arrogance on the outside, we have crossed the line. There is absolutely nothing wrong with valuing yourself highly and believing you can and will accomplish anything you set out to do. You should feel this way. What you do not have to do is tell everybody you meet about how great you are. Take Nike's advice, *"Just do it."* Go quietly and confidently on your journey.

Stop and Think: When you hear someone with conceit bragging on themselves about what they have done and are going to do, do you want to hear more? Do they have more or less influence?

One of the quickest ways to build trust is to get results. When you are meeting someone or a group for the first time, in order to influence them at a high level, you must do two things. You must build a relationship with them based on your character (who you are). Humility is key here. You must also let them know you are competent and have been successful in their area of interest. Results are key here. Getting results is a competency trait.

The quickest way to lose trust is through one of the character traits. Humility is weighted very heavily in the character equation. Little or no humility definitely lowers your trustworthiness. If you think it's about you, you are more likely to believe you deserve the credit more than someone else.

> *"Talent is God given. Be humble.*
> *Fame is man-given. Be grateful.*
> *Conceit is self-given. Be careful."*
> *~ John Wooden*

You may or may not be a person of faith, but you surely understand we are all born with a specific set of natural talents. We did not have to earn them.

Wooden said, *"Be humble."* You do not deserve the credit for your natural talent, it's a gift. So, don't try and take the credit. On fame, he said, *"Be grateful."* Fame can only be earned through influence. You cannot decide you are going to be famous, only others can choose to make you famous by recognizing you for good or bad. Wooden said it best at the end, *"Be careful."* He is talking about conceit. No one can make you conceited. You must choose to be conceited. You can also choose to be humble and avoid it. Either is a choice.

To better understand humility, let's look at what it is not. When someone chooses to be conceited, they are choosing arrogance, pride, and ego over humility. For these individuals, it is about power and recognition. It's not only about getting the credit, but also about taking the credit from others to boost their own ego.

They need the credit. They seize it. And, they feed upon it. Their influence, if they have any, typically comes through fear and intimidation manifested through a position of authority. This authority could be as a parent or a teacher. It could come from having rank or a title.

Without a position of authority and without resorting to violence, these people would not have very much influence. No one would want to follow them or do what they said do if they did not have to do it. These people get their influence from borrowing power and strength from their position or their authority.

If we're a manager, a boss, a parent, have higher rank, or have been granted formal authority over others, borrowing power from our position does not automatically make us a better leader than someone without a position. It can actually lower our level of influence if the power associated with the position is abused. People who *"have to"* follow us will not give us 100% effort. Instead, they will resent us and withhold the extra effort a humble leader would easily earn.

Nearly everyone has had a *"formal authority"* boss with low level moral influence. Formal authority is about power and position over others. Moral authority is about humility and earning influence with others while respecting them regardless of one's own position. One leader, we prefer not to be around or work with. The other, we love and appreciate. With high impact leadership (influence), we feel it more than we see it.

Whether you have a position of authority or not, if you want to increase your influence with others, the key is to develop strong, positive relationships based on your character and moral authority. Consider the motive behind a conceited person and a humble person. Why do they seek to influence? Their benefit or someone else's? What's their intent?

Stop and Think: If you know someone is influencing you only to boost their ego, are they building trust or creating distrust? Will they have more or less influence?

Stop and Think: If you know someone has your best interest at heart and will give you the credit for your success, are they building trust or creating distrust? Will they have more or less influence?

You will never find an arrogant, prideful, ego driven person serving others. You may absolutely find them using others in the name of service, but they will be found out eventually. Humility serves while conceit deserves.

Stop and Think: If someone's intent is to serve you, do they build trust or create distrust? Does their influence increase or decrease? Are they more likely to be humble or conceited?

Stop and Think: If someone's intent is to be served by you, do they build trust or create distrust? Does their influence increase or decrease? Are they more likely to be humble or conceited?

"We have to humble ourselves and the way we do that is by serving other people." ~ Tim Tebow

10

CHARACTER LEVERAGES COMPETENCY

Character Will Take Us Most of the Way; Competency Will Take Us the Rest of the Way

"Most people don't lead their life. They accept their life."
~ John Cotter

There is no doubt that our character is most important when it comes to developing our influence. But, character can only take us so far. We must develop our competency in order to reach our full potential. We have infinite potential relative to improving our character and competency.

Merriam-Webster's definition of competency:
- an ability or skill

Once you have developed your character and are able to influence people who want to follow you, where are you going to lead them? Nowhere, unless you develop your competency. You must learn and develop skills and talents. Others will place value on who you are (character) and what you know (competency).

There are numerous ways to develop your competency. You can start in an entry level position within an organization and learn on-the-job. You can self-educate by reading, learning, and applying. You can go to a technical college to learn a trade or enroll in a traditional college to earn one or more degrees. Or, you may join a branch of the military receiving your formal training through the military's many formal and technical schools combined with on-the-job training.

Character leads to relationships while competency leads to results. Without character, there will be no relationship. Without competency, there will be no results. To be highly effective, we need character and competency. Once you have influence with others through your character development, you must have a skill set to pair it with in order to produce results.

TALENTS

Merriam-Webster's definition of talent:
- a special ability allowing someone to do something well

Where should you start, or for some, where should you restart. The best place to start is to tap into your natural talents, the abilities you came preloaded with at birth. You may have already identified them and likely have been recognized for them. However, you may not be utilizing them and maximizing them to your full benefit.

I have heard during my professional training sessions, *"If you were to take a group of 10,000 people and fully develop their natural talents, every person could do something better than anyone else."* You can develop your natural talents much easier and quicker than you can develop your unnatural talents. The problem is many people never develop their natural talents.

One of my natural talents is leadership (influence). I remember the evening I met Ria on June 16, 2000. I was talking to a group of guys, one of which I worked with and knew well. Ria and her friend Autumn walked up and started talking to the group.

I was attracted to her as soon as I saw her. I thought if she knew the guys in the group I would already have a head start. Being part of the group, I would be able to get to know her by borrowing influence from them. Influencing others has always been a natural talent for me. However, it was many years before I focused on developing this natural talent.

She and Autumn talked briefly to the group before walking away. As soon as they were gone, I told my friend, *"Ria is definitely going to get a chance to turn me down later."* It was love at first sight. At least, it was for me. She didn't have an interest in me, but she had noticed me. I had work to do.

All I had to do was find an opportunity to leverage the group's influence in order to connect with her. We ended up talking later that evening. After an hour or so, it was time to leave. I gave her my cell number, my email address, and left it up to her to contact me. Two weeks later, we were on our first date. We married 16 months later on October 27, 2001.

At the time, I didn't realize I was using leadership principles to meet her. I was not using them to lead a team or group to accomplish a noble mission, but I was using them to build relationships. Because of weaknesses in my character in those days, no one would have been willing to pay me to teach leadership principles. My natural talents were very raw and undeveloped, but I still had them.

Unfortunately, we can influence positively and negatively. Until I focused on my character development, my influence was all over the place. I wasn't aware of the potential positive use of my natural talents and abilities until I started studying leadership in 2008 which quickly exposed my passion for it as well.

Everyone has natural talents and abilities waiting to be discovered. We should continue to grow and develop our natural talents endlessly. How do we do it? We must experiment.

When is the last time you did something for the first time? Try something new. Don't forget about those character traits we discussed: courage, perseverance, and confidence. Those traits may lead you to unleash the untapped natural talents and abilities you may not realize you possess.

What do you do for fun? What are your hobbies? If you could pick any job and pay was not a concern, what would it be? These are good places to start exploring.

KNOWLEDGE

Merriam-Webster's definition of knowledge:
- information, understanding, or skill you get from experience or education

"Some leaders feel that by keeping their people in the dark, they maintain a measure of control. But that is a leader's folly and an organization's failure. Secrecy spawns isolation, not success. Knowledge is power, yes, but what leaders need is collective power, and that requires collective knowledge."
~ Captain D. Michael Abrashoff

Another way to develop your competency is to increase your knowledge. One of my favorite books is *Think and Grow Rich.* In his early 1900s book, Napoleon Hill writes about generalized and specialized knowledge.

"General knowledge, no matter how great in quantity or variety it may be, is of but little use in the accumulation of money. The faculties of the great universities possess, in the aggregate, practically every form of general knowledge known to civilization. Most of the professors have but little or no money. They specialize in teaching knowledge, but they do not specialize in the organization, or the use of knowledge." ~ Napoleon Hill

To put Hill's thoughts into context, he was studying the most wealthy and influential people of the early 20th century such as Henry Ford, Andrew Carnegie, Charles Schwab, John Rockefeller, Thomas Edison, Alexander Graham Bell, and many more. Therefore, professors may have earned decent salaries as they do today, but they were not in the same league as those Hill was studying and comparing them to. Professors, then and now, do not typically fit into the rich and highly influential category.

Hill's last statement is key, *"They specialize in teaching knowledge, but they do not specialize in the organization or use of knowledge."* If you do not have a formal education or college degree, you can still develop specialized knowledge. You do not necessarily need a degree from a university to be successful. There are numerous examples throughout our history of those without formal education acquiring great wealth through hard work, influence, and self-education.

Thomas Edison had only 12 weeks of formal education. He was age seven or eight when he received it. He was deemed too difficult to teach and was removed from school by his mother. However, he developed an appetite for knowledge and reading books at age 11. Hill said of Edison, *"He did not lack education, neither did he die poor."* Henry Ford had no more than a sixth grade formal education and created one of the top automotive manufacturing companies in the world.

Both men were highly educated but not formally educated. They both obtained a Ph.D. in results. Results are what matter. It does not matter where or how the education to achieve the results is obtained. Where you develop your education is irrelevant in comparison to what you're able to do with it once you have it.

"Knowledge has no value except that which can be gained from its application toward some worthy end." ~ *Napoleon Hill*

Getting results is much more important than getting a degree. Otherwise, what value is the knowledge you have? You must be able to leverage your knowledge before you will be able to benefit from having the knowledge.

In Napoleon Hill's time, less than 30% of people graduated from high school. Today, nearly 80% of people graduate high school and a large number of them continue straight into college. Unfortunately, whether they graduate from high school or college, many of them finish intentionally acquiring knowledge once their formal education ends.

"For years, people have recognized the value of a four-year degree, but to succeed in today's economy, you really need a 40 year degree." ~ *Stephen M. R. Covey*

If you want to stick out in today's society, get major results, and sail your way to success while everyone else is struggling to stay afloat, you must do more than develop your character. You must leverage your character in order to intentionally develop specialized knowledge in your area of interest. You may want to consider picking up additional books related to character development and to the competencies where you have an interest. Or, you may want to enroll in a formal program to further develop yourself.

It takes very little effort to stand out in today's society. Many people in school or college cannot wait to get finished, get a job, move away from intentional learning, and get comfortable.

With self-discipline, those continuing to educate themselves intentionally by developing their specialized knowledge steadily and consistently increase their potential to do more, earn more, and be more. They also do more than get results. They become even more valuable to society as they begin to help others get results.

"Successful people, in all callings, never stop acquiring specialized knowledge related to their major purpose, business, or profession. Those who are not successful usually make the mistake of believing that the 'knowledge-acquiring' period ends when one finishes school. The truth is that formal education does but little more than to put one in the way of learning how to acquire practical knowledge." ~ Napoleon Hill

SKILLS

Merriam-Webster's definition of skill:
- the ability to do something that comes from training, experience, or practice

"The man who will use his skill and constructive imagination to see how much he can give for a dollar, instead of how little he can give for a dollar, is bound to succeed." ~ Henry Ford

We tend to think of knowledge as something we know and a skill as something we do. Skills and talents are very similar. Talents are something you're good at and can do naturally, while skills must be developed through training and education.

Many skills are taught in a classroom type setting beginning with an orientation covering the basic knowledge and understanding required to master the skill. Often, the classroom training transitions to hands-on, experiential training. A few examples are: electrician, welder, mechanic, attorney, air conditioning technician, pilot, physician, and many other positions in the medical field.

Some skills are not taught in the classroom. Instead, they are learned through hands-on, experiential training only. This is often referred to as on-the-job training. There are many blue-collar jobs like this across many different industries. A few examples are: machine operation, carpentry, masonry, and equipment operation. Training can also begin in the classroom, but far too often it doesn't.

You do not need to be naturally talented in an area to develop a related skill. Sure, you must put in extra effort compared to someone who has the natural talent, but you can often learn to do it as well or better than those with a natural ability.

How can you outperform someone who has natural talent in a given area? It's because they are happy with their natural abilities and never put in the extra effort to become exceptional in their area of giftedness.

Developing your talents, knowledge, and skills in the areas where you have the greatest interest complements your character and increases your influence with people sharing the same interest.

STYLE

Merriam-Webster's definition of style:
- a particular way in which something is done, created, or performed

When you merge your character and competency your unique leadership style is revealed. Your style is how you interact with others while you're doing what you do. Your style determines how you use your influence in an effort to motivate and inspire others to take action. Some people may have a calm and soothing style that attracts others to them. Some may have a harsh and dictatorial style that repels others away from them. Others may find themselves somewhere in between.

There are as many styles as there are people because each person's combination of character, experience, and competency is unique to them.

A negative style of leadership is a direct result of poor character. When you begin to intentionally develop your character, the first thing people will notice is a change in your leadership style, the way you attempt to influence others. If your leadership style already appeals to others with well-developed character and increases your influence with them, it's because of your previous character development.

"Great leaders are almost always great simplifiers who offer a solution everybody can understand." ~ General Colin Powell

If we want everyone to be part of the solution instead of being part of the problem, we need to talk *to* everyone and talk *above* no one. Talking to a few while talking above many is a weak leadership style at best. It always takes more energy to connect with more people. If our objective is to accomplish the mission, no one needs to be impressed but everyone needs to be involved.

Stop and Think: Which person would you trust most, someone trying to impress you or someone trying to connect with you? Which person would have more influence?

When it comes to style, keep this in mind: you are always working for *yourself*, not someone else. You may work at someone else's organization and someone else may be paying you, but you are always working for *yourself*. Even if you own your business, someone else is always paying you. They are called the customer.

It's no different when you work inside of someone else's organization, but for some reason, the person paying you is called the boss instead of the customer. However, your boss is your most important customer. Why? You are always working for *yourself*. This is why *who you are* and *what you know* is so important. Your entire future depends on YOU. You determine the quality and quantity of your customers.

If we are working for ourselves, everyone we serve is our customer. The style of the person who views someone paying them as the boss is different than the style of someone who sees them as their customer. Our style has a direct effect on our influence.

The best form of advertisement is word of mouth. If we are always working for ourselves, what kind of word of mouth advertisement are we getting from our customers every day?

Change your perspective. Change your style. Change your results.

RESULTS

Merriam-Webster's definition of results:
-   something that is caused by something else that happened or was done before

"I was not interested in flattery or fluff. Rigidity gets in the way of creativity. Instead of salutes, I wanted results."
~ *Captain D. Michael Abrashoff*

Our character and competency determine our cumulative influence which determines our results. Results are how we quantify and measure the effectiveness of our leadership (influence). The fastest way to build trust is to get results. When we build trust, we gain influence by increasing the confidence others have in us.

Would you like to go to work every day and not be bossed by anyone? You would still have someone tell you what's expected, but no one would boss you. Most people are quick to say how great it would be, but they think it's not realistic.

If you don't want anyone to boss you, you must simply achieve the desired results. Do things before you are expected to do them. Do more than you are expected to do. Do things better than you are expected to do them. Over deliver and you will be appreciated, and your influence will increase. You will be seen as an exceptional and valued team member. You won't have a boss. You'll have a cheerleader.

Getting results means taking full responsibility:

> We cannot say, *"I don't think it will work."*
> We must say, *"I will make it work."*
> We cannot say, *"Well, I tried it, and it didn't work."*
> We must say, *"I found a way to make it work."*

We must get it done. We must make things happen. Getting results means we don't complain. The more we complain, the less we obtain. At the end of the day, someone has to make it happen, why not you?

> *"Helping your boss when he or she needs you badly is a pretty good investment."* ~ Captain D. Michael Abrashoff

Stop and Think: Do you trust someone getting results more or less than someone trying to get results? Which person would have more influence?

Your results matter. Did you get results in the past? Are you currently getting the desired results? Are you constantly growing your character and competency with the intent of producing better results in the future at a higher level? What will you be able to do one, five, or 10 years down the road that you aren't doing now? Will you produce less, the same, or more results in the future?

> *"Your time is limited, so don't waste it living someone else's life. Don't be trapped by dogma - which is living with the results of other people's thinking. Don't let the noise of others' opinions drown out your own inner voice. And most important, have the courage to follow your heart and intuition."* ~ Steve Jobs

11

DEFINING YOUR LEADERSHIP STYLE

Get Out of the Way and Lead

"Coaches that can outline plays on a blackboard are a dime a dozen, but the ones that can succeed are the ones that can get inside their players and motivate them." ~ Vince Lombardi

Why do people choose to follow a leader? There are many reasons. Here are three:

1. They do not trust the leader and are afraid not to follow. – They are afraid they may not get something they want such as: time off, a raise, or a promotion they want. They may be afraid something bad will happen to them such as: being demoted, being assigned to a job they don't want to do, being told to work hours or days they don't want to work, or being fired.

2. They have limited trust in the leader and believe they may benefit in some way. – If they do what they are asked, they believe good things will happen to them such as: keeping their job, getting raises, receiving time off, receiving recognition, receiving promotions, receiving additional responsibilities, etc.

3. They fully trust the leader. – They believe the leader wants to help them. They believe the leader cares about their well-being. They believe

the leader has good character based on what they have witnessed. They believe the leader has the knowledge and skills to lead the team.

When interacting with people, it is important to understand the difference between managing people (directing, controlling) and leading people (influencing, releasing). Considering the three reasons people follow a leader, no trust and limited trust occur when people are being *managed* by a self-serving leader. Fully trusting occurs when people are being *led* by a servant leader.

Choosing how and when to use management techniques and leadership principles will play a major role in determining your style and your level of effectiveness relative to influencing people.

We must *manage* things and processes, but we should *lead* people. We obviously cannot lead (influence) things and processes. Things and processes cannot think. Things and processes do not have feelings. Things and processes do not choose to follow. We must make decisions about things and processes and take action to achieve the related desired results. Or, we must influence others to take action on our behalf.

We can make the mistake of attempting to manage people by treating them like objects while using control, power, and authority in an effort to get them to do what we say should be done, when we say it should be done, and how we say it should be done. It happens at work and at home when someone has a position of authority and the rights to direct the actions of others. It's fast, but it's not highly effective.

If we want to be served by people, we manage them. If we want to serve people, we lead them. When it comes to leadership, it's more caught than taught.

People with formal authority over others are

commonly referred to as managers and have a position in management such as: manager, boss, supervisor, director, vice-president, president, or owner. Relative to the military, they simply have higher rank. Having formal authority does not mean someone is a good manager or a good leader. It means they have been given formal authority to make decisions and the right to lead and to direct the work of others. Some are great leaders. Many are extremely poor, low impact leaders, and everyone following them is aware of it.

Many people are curious how low impact leaders are able to remain in their position. It's because those reporting to them have not developed themselves and do not have other options. If they had other options, they would act on them. Then, if those filling the vacancy had options, they would act too when the poor leader revealed their true character.

A low impact leader can only lead because people without options *have to* follow. Otherwise, the low impact leader would not have anyone to lead. Low impact leaders, like high impact leaders, can only lead when someone chooses to follow. Low impact followers without options follow and enable low impact leaders. It's that simple.

Instead of taking the initiative and responsibility to develop themselves, those following poor leaders tend to blame the leader. Why? It's easy. Those blaming do not have to do anything to improve their circumstances. They feel it is the leader's fault they are miserable and being mistreated. Nothing is farther from the truth. Our problem is always in the mirror (self). It's never through the window (others).

If I'm following a low impact, controlling, dictatorial leader, it's not their fault. It's my fault. They cannot stop me from taking responsibility, developing myself, creating options, and removing myself from the situation. Only I can do that. If I will not pay the price to create more and better options for myself, it's not someone else's fault. It's my fault.

If you want to be more effective and learn about the underlying principles needed to give yourself more options, get a copy of *The 7 Habits of Highly Effective People* by Stephen R. Covey. Reading it will raise your self-awareness. However, in order to reap the benefits, you must learn to apply the principles daily. If you do, your life will change, and you will create more options.

Early in my career, I had to follow low impact leaders. I was always frustrated. I was bad mouthing them along with nearly everyone else who had to follow them. I hated going to work. Not because of the job, but because of the boss. At least, that's what I thought because of my low level of awareness. I was a low impact follower. I didn't apply myself. I didn't have options. And, I chose to be frustrated.

"The number one reason people leave their jobs is a bad relationship with their boss." ~ Stephen M. R. Covey

Low impact followers usually stay and continue blaming their boss for their bad circumstances. High impact followers usually leave because they have more options and know they are responsible for removing themselves from the situation if they don't like it.

You can always develop yourself and no longer have to work for or with anyone you feel does not respect you or the team. Is it easy? Most of the time, it's not. Is it possible? Every single time it is, if you are willing to pay the price to grow and develop yourself.

If you want to *change* your world, you must first change *your* world. To clarify, if you want to change your environment, you who are living in the environment, must first change.

"We are anxious to improve our circumstances but unwilling to improve ourselves. We therefore remain bound." ~ James Allen

Until you apply what you've learned, nothing changes. Deciding to do something and doing it are two very different things delivering very different results.

Do not assume the misuse of formal authority only happens at work. It happens at home with parents trying to control and manage their children by using their formal authority to force or coerce them into complying through fear, intimidation, and discipline. It can also happen at home between the adults when one or both of them try to control and manage the other.

If we think our spouse and children are there to serve us, we manage them. If we think we are there to serve our spouse and children, we lead them.

There is only one reason anyone responds or complies when being managed. They *have to*. If they did not *have to*, they wouldn't. You may have been there at some point in your life when you had to follow someone only because they had a position of authority or power over you. Most of us have been there.

Stop and Think: When someone tries to control you with force or coerce you with fear, intimidation, and discipline, do they build trust or create distrust? Do they have more or less influence?

Management of people reflects low impact

117

leadership and results in low level effectiveness. It is the lowest form of influence. Managing is directing from a position of authority. Leading is influencing through character-based, moral authority with or without a position.

People do not like to be managed. Anytime people are being managed there is low trust and resistance. People like to be led by people with strong, positive character. We not only need to be great at managing things and processes and leading people, but we also need to know when to use the skills and principles associated with each practice.

Stop and Think: When dealing with people, are you a manager or a leader? Which person builds more trust? The one directing and controlling or the one leading and influencing? Which one would you prefer to follow?

You have likely seen the results of someone without formal authority trying to manage someone else at home or at work. Usually, both parties become frustrated which leads to ruptured relationships. When you don't have formal authority or power over someone, there is only one way to move them to action. You must establish moral authority before you can influence them.

If you have a desire to become a principle-centered leader, you must learn to lead with influence, regardless of whether or not you currently have a position of authority. If you do not currently have a position of authority or power, you can only lead based on the relationships you have developed because you have not been given formal authority or the rights associated with leading others. However, if you don't have a position of authority but continue to grow and develop your influence with others, it will only be a matter of time before you are offered one.

If this happens and you accept a formal position of authority, remember, your current relationships were built without authority. Everything will instantly be reset. You must understand the existing relationships will not automatically continue at the same level once you're given a position of authority. You must rebuild or confirm your relationships on top of your new position. Often, it will be harder than before.

Others may become suspicious of your intent. Most importantly, when you have authority and power over others, things will feel and be different. You may act differently toward them. They may begin to see you differently too. You will no longer have to be patient. You will be able to control others and force compliance at your pace if you choose.

The key to leading with moral authority is based on your ability to build trust with or without a position. Before you can begin, you must establish your intent by truly seeking mutual benefit with others. They must believe there is a benefit for them if they are going to voluntarily choose to follow you in your new position.

Once you have established trust based on *character*, you must establish trust based on *competency* in order to lead others to achieve the desired results. After you have a proven track record others can verify, you will be able to choose to make the necessary sacrifices to further develop your influence and begin to help others learn to lead based on their relationships and to get their own results.

Leaders getting results effectively based on strong,

solid relationships do not make a habit of mistreating and disrespecting those following them. They seek mutual respect. This is a *good* place to be as a leader.

However, the majority of good leaders do not go the extra mile and become *great* leaders. In order to climb to the next level, they must invest time and resources into the people following them with the sole purpose of helping them increase their influence and helping them get better results.

High impact leaders have an abundance mindset. They invest in their team. They think many, many options. There is plenty of everything for everyone. There is plenty of credit for everyone, plenty of profit for everyone, plenty of room for everyone to grow, and plenty of opportunity for everyone.

They know, if they invest in the people, the entire team's cumulative influence increases. They are secure and share information freely.

They know: **T**ogether **E**veryone **A**chieves **M**ore. High impact leaders with an abundance mindset help others succeed because they are not threatened by their success.

They invest heavily in developing their team because they know they must grow the team to grow the organization. As the team grows, they know trust increases, speed increases, costs decrease, profits increase, quality improves, and morale improves.

People with an abundance mindset build more trust with others, and they do it quicker. They have an abundance of influence and focus heavily on developing the character and competency of their team members.

Low impact leaders have a scarcity mindset. They think there is only so much to go around. They place a priority on making sure they get their share. They are insecure in their position within the organization and feel threatened by others at all levels. Therefore, they hoard information and guard their turf. They do not want to develop their team beyond what is required. Leaders with a scarcity mindset are fearful of training their team members. They believe trained team members may leave the organization or threaten their position in the future. Therefore, they do not invest in the growth of the team. As a result, the organization cannot grow. These leaders tend to blame the team for the poor results instead of taking the blame. They are experts at dodging and transferring responsibility.

When it comes to training people, those with a scarcity mindset think, *"What happens if we train them, and they leave?"* So, they don't train their team. However, there is something far worse than training people who leave. What's worse? Not training them and having them stay. People come and go whether being trained or not, but they are more likely to stay longer if they feel valued by their leader.

Stop and Think: Which organization would you trust more? One with abundance seeking growth throughout while training and developing their team? Or, one with scarcity struggling to maintain the status quo and isn't training and developing their team? Which would earn more of your loyalty? Which would attract and retain better team members?

When it comes to the activity in an organization, leaders are making it happen (good or bad), allowing it to happen (good or bad), or preventing it from happening (good or bad). Ultimately, the top leader is responsible whether they accept responsibility or not.

High impact leaders take responsibility for what is or isn't happening. Low impact leaders avoid taking responsibility for what is or isn't happening as they search for others to blame. They create a tremendous amount of distrust throughout the organization as they try to maintain power and control while attempting to transfer responsibility.

It takes a lot of character development to become a high impact leader because you must move beyond only accepting responsibility for growing yourself. When you truly and sincerely begin to develop and grow others, you also become responsible to others, not just for others. Low impact leaders are unwilling to do this. They have the ability, but they do not have the desire.

If you invest abundantly in others, your influence will exponentially increase through them.

The 5 Types of Leaders

Type 1: Managerial Leader

- Character is weak; desire is *"to be served"* rather than *"to serve;"* scarcity mindset
- Competency can range from undeveloped to highly developed
- Focus is on managing (directing and controlling) people and processes
- Values the position more than the people
- Strength comes from power, control, formal authority, personal results

A *managerial* leader is the least effective of the five types of leaders. They have the least influence. People only follow them because they have to. They are not in the position to serve others. Their desire is to be served by others because they are in the position. They see others as tools to use to complete their objective. They prefer to make decisions. Their weakness is character development.

Type 2: Relational Leader

- Character is strong; desire is to serve; abundance mindset
- Competency is undeveloped, generalized
- Focus is on leading (influencing and releasing) people
- Values people more than their position
- Strength comes from relationships and moral authority

A *relational* leader builds relationships in order to influence others. People want to follow them because of who they are, not what they know. They develop mutual respect with others and work well with them. Although people want to follow them, they have not developed specialized knowledge. Their weakness is not making the necessary sacrifices to develop their competency.

Type 3: Motivational Leader

- Character is strong; desire is to serve; abundance mindset
- Competency is developed, specialized
- Focus is on leading (influencing and releasing) people, managing the processes, and getting results

- Values people more than their position
- Strength comes from relationships, moral authority, and team results

A *motivational* leader seeks mutual benefit for themselves, others, and the organization. People want to follow them because of who they are and what they know. They influence others from the outside. They are process focused. They are trusted and deliver results for themselves, their families, their team, their organization, their customers, their suppliers, and their community. Their weakness is not making the necessary sacrifices to reproduce other motivational leaders.

Type 4: Inspirational Leader

- Character is stronger; desire is to serve and develop others; abundance mindset
- Competency is highly developed, specialized
- Focus is on leading (influencing and releasing) people and developing motivational leaders
- Values people more than their position
- Strength comes from relationships, moral authority, and the growth and success of others

An *inspirational* leader inspires managerial and relational leaders to become motivational leaders. Their focus is on growing themselves in order to inspire others to grow. They influence others on the inside. They are people focused not process focused. They focus heavily on character development. True inspirational leaders are followed because of how much they care and who they are on the inside. They are inspired by the growth of those following them.

Type 5: Transformational Leader

- Character is strongest; desire is to serve and to develop others; abundance mindset
- Competency is highly developed, specialized
- Focus is on leading (influencing and releasing) people and developing motivational and inspirational leaders
- Values people more than their position
- Strength comes from relationships, moral authority, growth and success of others, and the respect they have earned

A *transformational* leader's passion and purpose is to transform others. They are the most influential of the five types of leaders and are highly respected. Their reputation precedes them. They are well known for developing high impact leaders. Their influence touches people within all industries and across multiple generations. They have influenced many leaders for many years. Their influence is continuously being transferred through many other leaders at many different times in multiple locations.

As you consider the following examples, notice the *manager* style will correspond with the managerial type of leader. The *leader* style will correspond with one or more of the relational, motivational, inspirational, and transformational types of leaders which build strong relationships, get results for the people and the organization, and reinvest in people by growing and developing them to become highly effective leaders.

In my Lean Manufacturing Consulting business, I often taught the *"manager vs. leader"* principles I'm about to share with you in order to help the team leaders understand how to better lead the continuous improvement teams effectively without formal authority. Most of the time they didn't have any. Or, if they did, they attempted to leverage it too much which quickly shut down the team, caused friction, limited buy-in, limited results, and decreased the team's overall effectiveness.

Since then, I have enhanced it. This comparison is very effective in helping others see the difference between the two styles. A perspective on the leader is included in each category.

Managing People vs. Leading People

Vision

Manager: Focus is short-term. Expects subordinates to also focus on the short-term. Primarily concerned with today.

Leader: Focus is long-term. Expects followers to also focus on the long-term. Primarily concerned with the future.

Leaders (people of influence) are responsible for establishing the vision and looking at the big picture whether it is for their family, their team, their department, or their business. Leaders should focus on doing what no one else can or will do. If they don't do it, it's not likely to get done. Leaders cast the vision.

"Vision is foresight with insight based on hindsight."
~ John C. Maxwell

Change

Manager: Expects things to stay the same. Focus is on stability and control in an effort to maintain the status quo. Does not solicit or appreciate opinions of others relative to making things better in the future. Avoids, dislikes, and resists change.

Leader: Understands things will and should change. Focus is on leading change and releasing others to continuously make improvements. Solicits the ideas and opinions of others in order to facilitate improvements. Expects, embraces, and leverages change.

Leaders always seek a better way to do everything. Many leadership skills are needed in order to effectively lead continuous change. There will be challenges along the way. People need strong, growing leaders to take them, the team, the family, or the organization to the next level.

Self

Manager: Concerned with managing the work being done. Span of control is limited because of a micro-management style. Always checking up on, *snoopervising*, and hovering over those doing the work. They feel others will not come through without supervision. Drags or pushes people along because they are not following and complying willingly.

Leader: Concerned with leading and developing the people doing the work. Span of influence is significant because it is multiplied through others. Always has faith others will follow through and is confident they will accomplish the mission. Comes alongside the people to help them achieve success.

Leaders continually grow in order to grow and develop others. To do big things, a big team is needed. The size of the team is determined by the size of the leader. They must bring together and lead people with various skills, energy levels, and natural talents. They are continuously sharpening their leadership skills to become highly effective.

Others

Manager: Sees people reporting to them as subordinates serving the manager while carrying out the mission. Wants the people to accomplish the mission without support.

Leader: Sees people reporting to them as paid volunteers who should be respected, served, and supported. Wants to support the people in order to help them accomplish the mission.

Leaders valuing people have the primary goal of serving others. This means staying with the people, not leaving them behind while enjoying the spoils of success. A leader must be able to climb to the top of the mountain. However, a high impact leader will not remain there enjoying the view alone. They will go back down and help others climb their way to success. It's not about how far they can advance themselves, but how far they can advance others.

Power

Manager: Values *"rights"* associated with their formal authority and position. Utilizes positional authority to dictate, control, coerce, and order people to action.

Leader: Values influence established through their character development. Builds strong relationships and trust in order to motivate and move people to action.

A high impact leader with formal authority chooses to lead with influence not authority. Doing so generates a tremendous amount of trust with those reporting to them. When the leader can lead with an iron fist but chooses to lead with a warm heart, it does not go unnoticed. It gets talked about, and it gets appreciated. A leader knows life is hard, so they deliver easy. Those following this type of leader are very loyal and consistently over deliver with exceptional results.

Decision Making

Manager: Wants to make decisions for the people. Does not welcome the input of others. Does not ask many questions. Prefers to give answers.

Leader: Wants to facilitate decision making by the people. Welcomes input from others. Values the opinions and ideas of others. Asks many questions. Wants to help others find their own answers.

A high impact leader leads by not only asking questions, but also by expecting to be questioned which clearly communicates pride and ego are not an issue.

This leader highlights the importance of teamwork and shared results. They know they do not know it all. They do not expect others to know it all. They respect the opinions and the ideas of those closest to the work.

"It's what you learn after you know it all that counts."
~ John Wooden

Energy Source

Manager: Thrives on control. Gives orders to move others to action. Is most excited when they are in control making things happen through the manipulation of others.

Leader: Exhibits passion. Motivates and inspires others to take action. Is most excited when they are able to influence others to take initiative and make things happen.

This type of leader is always self-motivated. They know if they cannot motivate themselves to action, they will never be able to motivate and inspire others to action. They make things happen. Their energy and drive is contagious and spreads to those around them.

Risk

Manager: Seeks to minimize and avoid risks at all costs. Afraid of failing.

Leader: Takes calculated risks after consulting with others. Understands taking risks leads to learning and growth. Expects to fail as a way of learning.

High impact leaders are risk takers. They know if they already know how to do it, they won't grow while doing it. They have a hunger for risk. They know taking risks creates more opportunity. They don't take risks for the sake of taking risks. They take smart risks. To everyone else, it looks like they are out on a limb. To the leader, it is simply the next step on their journey to the next level and beyond.

"The problem is not that people aim too high and miss. The problem is that people aim too low and hit!" ~ Les Brown

Conflict

Manager: Avoids conflict, allows conflict to weaken relationships, and hopes it will be resolved without intervention. Believes all conflict is bad. Allows conflict to get out of control.

Leader: Uses conflict to build relationships, quickly resolves conflict, and mentors others to mitigate future conflict. Believes constructive conflict can be good.

When problems in the family or the organization arise, high impact leaders quickly pull everyone together and resolve the issue in a positive manner facilitating growth. Low impact leaders will be less effective when they attempt to lead others through conflict because they have not done the required self-development work in advance. If a leader can't help others resolve conflict, they need to take a look in the mirror and ask, *"What do I not know or not do that I need to know or do in order to fully support those needing my leadership during conflict?"* Humility is the key. Leadership equals responsibility.

Concern

Manager: Strong desire to *be right.* Does not like to be challenged. Quickly becomes defensive when they are questioned by others. Pride and ego guide them.

Leader: Strong desire to *do what is right.* Encourages others to stand up for what they believe. Intentionally synergizes with others in order to verify what is right. Humility strengthens them.

High impact, secure leaders excel in this area. They do not worry about being wrong. The only thing they concern themselves with is doing what's right. They don't care who provides the information needed to help them do the right thing. Their only concern is with getting the right information and taking the right action. Being approachable is a key character trait for leaders in this area.

Growth

Manager: Grows slowly and accidently through day to day activities while reaching goals set by others. Avoids intentional growth beyond what is required.

Leader: Grows quickly and intentionally by setting and developing goals for themselves and others. Seeks growth beyond what is required.

These leaders grow the organization by growing the people. They know the only way they can grow the people is to first grow themselves. Strong leaders in this area are always reading, attending seminars, watching videos, or listening to audios to further develop their character and competency. These leaders are out front sharing and teaching others what they're learning.

Credit

Manager: Quickly *"looks in the mirror"* and takes credit for what others have done when things go right. Driven by pride and ego.

Leader: Quickly *"looks through the window"* and gives credit freely to others when things go right. Demonstrates humility.

Everyone loves being around a leader excelling in this area. High impact leaders are always giving credit to others, sometimes credit they may rightly deserve themselves. They do not want it. They do not need it. They do not like it. What do these leaders like instead? Results! Everyone else can have the credit for the results. This leader simply wants the results and is happy to pass on the credit for achieving them to others.

Blame

Manager: Quickly *"looks through the window"* and blames others when things go wrong. Transfers responsibility.

Leader: Quickly *"looks in the mirror"* and takes the blame when things go wrong. Takes responsibility.

A leader that's quick to give the credit to others is usually the same one that will quickly take the blame.

People love this leader. No matter what goes wrong, this leader is quick to reflect and asks, *"What could I have done differently to prevent this? How was it my fault? What did I miss?"* They take the blame leaving everyone else in a position to move forward and get on with the task at hand.

Direction

Manager: Seeks to travel on existing roads put in place by others. Seeks what is comfortable and familiar.

Leader: Seeks to travel and explore new paths. Is a trailblazer. Seeks growth outside their comfort zone.

This leader simply says no to the status quo. They expect others to do the same. They are always looking for new ways to do things. Not for the sake of it being new, but for the sake of finding a better way. They like a challenge. They often help foster an atmosphere of experimentation where everyone feels safe to try new things. The leader knows if it does not work they can always go back to the way it was and try again. The key is to continuously be striving to get better.

Comfort Zone

Manager: Seeks to remain comfortable. Does not desire to grow. Is not comfortable when others are growing. Avoids those who are growing.

Leader: Is most comfortable being uncomfortable. Understands all growth happens outside the comfort zone. Associates with those consistently growing.

These leaders avoid comfort because they know, if they are comfortable, they are not growing. If they are comfortable, they know they are simply coasting to a stop. They are always on the go and always on the grow. They realize the more they know, the more they don't know. They have developed the mindset of continual growth and development. They don't waste time doing nothing when they can be doing something.

Responsibility

Manager: Takes a reactive approach. Blames others. Avoids taking responsibility. Transfers responsibility.

Leader: Takes a proactive approach. Blames self. Takes responsibility. Realizes they are either making things happen, allowing things to happen, or preventing things from happening.

When things go wrong on this leader's watch, they know there is only one reason it has happened: lack of leadership. They know responsibility lies with them. As a high impact leader, they have the ability to influence everything in the family or organization. These leaders always search their character first knowing most likely their own character flaw had a direct or indirect impact on what went wrong.

Speed

Manager: Makes decisions alone. As a result, they go fast in the beginning, but they go slow in the end as they try to gain buy-in and support from others. They are slow to solve problems because they don't involve others.

Leader: Makes decisions with others. As a result, they quickly gain buy-in, gather more ideas, and receive more support on the frontend which allows them to go much faster in the long run.

A leader knows it's not how fast they get started but rather how well they run the race that matters most. Leaders take the time to understand others and the situation in order to make sure their decisions are in alignment with reality. They take the time to ensure the right team members are involved. Instead of starting fast and going slow, they start slower and go faster.

"Take the time it takes, so it takes less time." ~ *Pat Parelli*

Stop and Think: Which is most effective a manager of people or a leader of people? Which would you trust more? Which would have the most influence?

WHERE
DO WE
INFLUENCE?

12

WHERE DO WE INFLUENCE?

Follow Your Passion to Find Your Purpose

"Look around you. Purpose is calling you from under rocks and in the hearts and souls of others. Someone out there needs you more than you need them!" ~ *Lt. General Hal Moore*

Unfortunately, many people will go to their grave never discovering their *why*. Instead, they will choose to settle for mediocrity instead of greatness. Why would anyone settle for mediocrity when they could have greatness? It's simple. It takes very little effort to be mediocre. However, it takes a lot of intentional effort to become exceptional. You must continually develop yourself, but it's worth it.

"When we discover what we are willing to pay a price for, we discover our life's mission and purpose." ~ *Kevin Hall*

Where will you have the greatest influence? Your area of passion is what determines where you have the greatest influence within yourself and with others. What motivates and inspires you gives you the energy and authenticity to motivate and inspire others. In order to fully leverage your passion to increase your influence, you must use it to discover, uncover, and refine your *why*. Your purpose.

"There are two great days in a person's life – the day you are born and the day you discover why." ~ *William Barclay*

Will you discover your purpose as you continue your journey through life? You may be thinking, *"What is my purpose?"* If so, you need to become intentionally focused on discovering what lies within you.

Finding your purpose sounds simple, but it's not. It requires a lot of discipline, stretching, risk taking, determination, and searching without settling. Too often in life, people who are searching find what they will settle for and stop looking for what they were searching for.

Discovering your purpose doesn't happen accidentally as you go through life. It happens intentionally as you grow through life. Once you discover and uncover your purpose, you cannot hide it from the rest of the world. You focus on it for the rest of your life. You slowly become one with your purpose.

Every day you grow intentionally is a day you discover more and learn more about your purpose.

"You will not grow without attempting things you are unable to do." ~ Henry Cloud

For me, discovering my purpose began with learning to intentionally sacrifice which is giving up something of lesser value today for something of greater value tomorrow or in the future. When you begin to discover your purpose, you will also begin to naturally value some things more than others. Then, those things of lesser value holding you back start to drop away. My transformation began when I started to read, learn, and literally apply what I was learning. Over and over and over again.

I am happy with where my journey has led me. Work has become play and play has become work. It's all the same. I read, learn, and apply to add value to myself, so I can then add value to others.

I started my intentional growth journey by following my passion to find my purpose. Leveraging your passion to find your purpose allows those needing and wanting your help to find you.

When you are operating with purpose as your driving force, you become exceptional. Someone *"just doing it"* cannot compete with someone *"loving to do it."*

No one can keep up with you. When you're doing what you love doing, your energy will be endless. You will stand out. You won't have a job. It's not something you just do. It's more. It's something you are.

Stop and Think: Who would you trust more to get the job done: someone doing what they do for money or someone passionate about it and driven to do it? Which person would have more influence?

Embracing my passion allowed me to find my purpose. I want to motivate and inspire you to embrace your passion, to find your purpose, and to unleash your true potential.

Our company, Top Story Leadership (originally founded as KaizenOps), exists to help people and organizations grow to where they had no idea they could go. Our mission is to unleash your team's potential by taking the complex and making it simple.

"The number one reason for lack of growth in people's lives is the absence of joining forces outside of themselves who push them to grow. Instead, they keep telling themselves that they will somehow, by willpower or commitment, make themselves grow. That never works." ~ Henry Cloud

Ria and I have made uncommon sacrifices to invest in our personal development and growth. By doing so, we have been modeling what we are teaching.

One way I keep lessons simple is through storytelling. I'm on this journey with you and want to share what finding my purpose has been like for me. I have applied and will always be applying the leadership principles I'm sharing with you in my own life.

Reading has the potential to significantly increase your value to others for a relatively low financial investment as a part of your intentional growth plan and should be aligned with your passion and purpose. The sacrifice is made, not only when you spend your money on the books, but also when you spend your time reading them and applying what you have learned from them.

High impact leaders intentionally read to succeed. If you're not reading, you're not leading. Leaders are readers. Leaders are learners. If you're not learning, you're not leading.

I first discovered my passion when I started achieving extraordinary results while leading cross-functional Lean Manufacturing process improvement teams. Then, my passion led me to my purpose: helping others grow and develop themselves for their own benefit and to accomplish their own mission. As I started to value my purpose more, others started to value me more.

Do you want to be successful? If so, do not focus on becoming successful. Focus on becoming more valuable. If you do, you will become highly successful. You will become most valued when you are driven by your passion and aligned with your purpose.

Growth is the path you must follow to become more

valuable. Growth of your character in areas of your weaknesses. Growth in your competency in areas of your strengths. If you are early in your career, you have a huge advantage. You have time on your side.

You may have already experienced great success. If so, please consider giving back to those needing your help. Not with dollars, but with a bigger sacrifice: time and knowledge. Write a book and share your story and successes humbly with the world. Be a lifter of others. If we're not lifting, we're loafing.

"There are people out there that will never be helped unless they hear your story. They can only be helped by you. They need to hear you and no one else." ~ Les Brown

I hope to inspire you to take action and allow your passion to lead you to your purpose. If I can do it, anyone can do it.

I barely graduated high school. I didn't attempt to apply myself. I was not focused on anything but graduating with the least amount of effort. I was leading myself at a low level and wasn't getting very much out of life with that type of attitude.

The person I used to be has moved out. He doesn't live inside of me anymore. A new me, with a new mission, has filled the vacancy.

When I was in school, I hated to read. So, I didn't. My grades reflected my choices. By the way, I still dislike reading. But, I have discovered learning leads to earning. We cannot give what we do not have. We cannot help others without first helping ourselves.

If you want to donate to your favorite charity, you must have it before you can give it. If you want to share knowledge with others, you must have it before you can share it. I've decided I like to learn more than I dislike reading. Therefore, I choose to read daily, on purpose to support my purpose.

What does society think about those who cannot read? I ask this question often and get these answers frequently: they are dumb, ignorant, stupid, lazy, and sometimes a few other harsh comments.

Don't forget. The people I'm referring to in the question have never learned how to read. They literally cannot read.

If we think this way about people who cannot read, what must we think about those who can read but choose not to read? Aren't they worse off? They have the ability but not the desire. As a result, they suffer the consequences of a self-imposed illiteracy.

Since they have never read regularly and frequently, they have never had a chance to see the results reading can bring. This is why I am going to share my personal story about reading and how applying what I have learned has impacted my life.

"The illiterate of the 21ˢᵗ century will not be those that cannot read or write but those that cannot learn, unlearn, and relearn."
~ Alvin Toffler

I suggest reading whether you like it or not. If you want to significantly increase your value, you must significantly add value to yourself. Reading *"junk"* content, not aligned with your passion and purpose, doesn't add value to you. You must read good books on something you are interested in doing, something you would like to do so much you would do it for free. Then, you must learn to do it so well people are willing to pay you to do it. Get in the zone and stay there.

I read a study some time ago stating, on average, no matter their career, people reading leadership books over a lifetime earned nearly three times more than those in the same field not reading leadership books. As their influence increased, so did their income.

No matter your passion and purpose, you must be able to positively influence people in order to add value to them and be valued by them. You must be able to influence them to voluntarily follow you.

Your influence determines where you go and when you go.

Stop and Think: When you hire someone to do something for you, does their character matter? Do you consider who they are (character) before you are concerned with what they know (competency)?

Stop and Think: If my character is outstanding but my competency is weak, does my lack of competency build trust or create distrust? Do I have more or less influence with you when compared to someone with outstanding character and strong competency?

If you read and learn the principles in one very good book, you will already be far ahead of those not reading. If you read a book a month for five years, you will have read 60 books. If you stay in your passion and purpose zone, you will be considered an expert by others. With discipline, it is easy to separate yourself from the crowd.

Stop and Think: Who would you trust and value more: someone with a four-year college degree and 10 years of accidental growth or someone without a college degree and 10 years of intentional growth who has read, learned, and applied the material from 100 or more books related to their passion and purpose? Which one would have more influence in their field? Which would have more confidence? Which one would have more competency in their field? What would happen to their influence if they had a four-year degree and had read a 100 or more books relative to their passion and purpose?

Most people don't come close to developing and reaching their full potential. They do enough to get comfortable and lose their desire to grow and stretch themselves any farther. I've read various surveys stating 30-40% of high school and college graduates never read another book.

We can easily move from average to exceptional. But, it won't just happen. We must make it happen. We must be intentional.

The key is to get into the minds of those already where you want to go. Those already doing what you want to do. You may know someone willing to mentor you in person or by phone. Either is great. As long as you are constantly growing your mind in the area of your passion and purpose, you cannot go wrong.

Humble people understand the more they learn, the more they realize what they haven't learned. They know they will never learn it all. They see the opportunities for growth ahead. They become lifetime learners and continue to run the race knowing there is no finish line.

While the ego-driven, prideful go through life thinking they have already crossed the finish line, the humble are like sponges soaking up a lifetime of knowledge because they are eager for growth. Who we are determines what we learn and how much we learn.

Don't focus on earning more. Focus on learning more. Increasing your value is a simple concept. It's not always easy to do, but it is always easy to understand.

Your value increases as you read, learn, and grow. It's a never ending process. Do not set a fixed goal and stop after reaching it. Understand your growth is infinite. Make your main goal continuous growth. Use small, short term goals to support the main goal.

We must make real sustainable changes if we are truly going to transform ourselves. In 2005, I changed the way I lived my life. The choice led me to my purpose. During my intentional growth journey, I changed something I did every day. I started reading every day in the area of my passion Lean Manufacturing and process improvement, which led me to eventually begin reading leadership development books.

There is no way I could have ever imagined the path I have taken. No matter where we are on our personal growth journey, we cannot fully imagine where we may end up in the future. We can never see too far ahead. We simply must start growing down the path.

"A year from now you may wish you had started today."
~ Karen Lamb

It's the same concept as the headlights on your car. Your lights only shine a short distance into the night, but you can drive endlessly. As you move forward, you're able to see what you could not see when you were sitting still. You must get going in order to see the path leading you to your destination.

Few people finish their formal education and continue to be intentional about learning. When we are through learning, we are through growing. Instead of learning, we are simply coasting and are depending on what we did in the past to take us into the future. If we leave our home planning to coast to our destination, we will never get far beyond where we started.

What you did to get you to where you are is what was needed to get you there, not what will take you to where you want to go. You must do more in order to go farther. Many finish high school or college, get a job, and *hope* to continue advancing endlessly. But a few, like you, actually do more. How much more is up to you. You can be assured what you do and how much you do will determine where you go and when you go.

Accidental on-the-job learning is what keeps your job, it is not what advances your career. It is what you get paid to do: the job. Accidental growth does not significantly increase your value. To increase your value, you must become intentional. Can you do it? Absolutely. The real question is, *"Will you do it?"* You're off to a good start. You're reading. You're already doing more than most people will ever do. Don't stop.

One way to consider the difference between accidental and intentional growth is to think about exercise. Most people can easily relate to exercise, whether they actually do it or not. What would your results be if you chose an accidental exercise plan versus an intentional exercise plan?

On the accidental plan, you don't do anything other than what is required, when it is required. Your fitness program is simply living your life day to day.

On the intentional plan, you consider where you are and where you want to be. You develop a strategy to get there through daily, intentional execution of the strategy. You track your progress and you make adjustments along the way.

It's no different with personal growth. We can do it accidentally or intentionally.

Ria has also applied leadership principles to discover her passion which is leading her toward her purpose. Doing so has allowed her to recently resign from her corporate job to join me in professional leadership development. How did she transition from being a waitress at a pizza restaurant in 2000, earning only a few dollars per hour, to become the Director of Regulatory Affairs at a large hospital? And then, resign to become a professional motivational leadership coach, trainer, speaker, and author in 2014? She became intentional about her growth and made it happen.

When I met her, she had no high school diploma or GED. Since then, she has earned an MBA with a 4.0 GPA. She did not coast after graduation as many do. Ria is a reader too. She started reading and studying leadership books to help her be a better leader at the hospital where she worked.

She didn't start growing with the intent of resigning. She thought she had found her passion and purpose in the medical industry. But as she grew, she found her passion was similar to mine. She developed the passion to help others unleash their potential. She is growing herself in order to better help others grow. She enjoys keynote speaking, professional coaching, and is currently writing books too.

Today, we spend our lives together doing what we love. One of our goals from the start has been to create the life we want instead of accepting the life we were given. It is no longer a goal. It is our reality. We became intentional about following our passion and found our purpose. There was a lot of sacrifice along the way. We have not arrived, but we are farther down the path.

We did not get to where we are because of our college degrees, but they did move us forward. Earning our college degrees allowed us to realize the value of intentional learning. We used our degrees to get demanding careers and didn't get to spend much time together as a result. So, we continued to be intentional and are where we are today because of the books we have read and continue to read since finishing college.

"Instead of wondering what your next vacation is, maybe you should set up a life you don't need to escape from." ~ Seth Godin

You may or may not believe you can do it. But, ask yourself, *"Is it possible?"* Yes, it's possible. To make it happen, you must take action. You must do what you know needs doing. You must do it when it needs to be done. Knowing how is not the key. Taking action is.

Where should you start?

1. Follow your conscience. What do you feel you should do? What do you want to do?
2. Consider your passion. What do you get excited about? What do you need to do?
3. Consider your natural talents. What are you naturally good at without much effort? What hobbies do you have? What interests you?
4. Consider what society needs and values. What do you love to do so much you would do it for free, but people are willing to pay others to do? What do you see others doing that you would like to do?

Find your *"happy"* spot where these questions overlap. Start reading books in this area. If this area requires a formal college education, make it happen. Get intentional and get the required education. Then, read. Read. Read. And, read some more. Be patient. You will slowly become an expert and have the most influence in the area where you invest the most time. Your world and your life will change in ways you cannot imagine as you continue down this path of personal growth on a quest to find your purpose.

No matter your passion and purpose. You should continue to read leadership books. To live your dream, you will need to influence many people to help you make it happen. Remember, leadership is influence. Nothing more. Nothing less. You cannot achieve your dream alone. You will need the assistance and cooperation of others.

Will it be easy? No. But, it *will* be worth it. You may suffer a few growing pains along the way as Ria and I did. I suspect there will always be more to come.

> *"Passion in its purest sense, the willingness to suffer for what we love, is often the door that leads us to our path."*
> ~ *Ralph Waldo Emerson*

If you travel the well-worn road to mediocrity, you will never find your purpose. You will never unleash your true potential and enjoy the rewards doing so will bring. However, you will find what you're willing to settle for in life which may not be what you want from life. But, it will be exactly what you are choosing in life.

Success is about me. Significance is about we.

If you want to find your purpose, you must get on the seldom traveled road toward significance that's filled with setbacks, roadblocks, obstacles, and detours. This road will lead you to your purpose. You must intentionally develop a vision of where you want to be in the future. Then, you must make a plan and start taking the steps that will move you from where you are to where you want to be. You should always be grateful for where you are and what you have accomplished, but you should never be satisfied.

"Vision is not enough. It must be combined with venture. It is not enough to stare up the steps; we must step up the stairs."
~ *Vaclav Havel*

WHO DO WE INFLUENCE?

13

WHO DO WE INFLUENCE?

If They Buy-In, They Are All In

*"Before you are a leader, success is all about growing yourself.
When you become a leader, success is all about growing others."*
~ *Jack Welch*

Once you have started to develop your influence,
who will you influence the most? You have the greatest
influence with those buying-in to you, those attracted to
who you are, and those interested in *what you know.* Only
those valuing and seeking what you value and seek will
volunteer to follow you. They give you or deny you
permission to influence them based on how well you
have developed your character and competency.

Without influence, you cannot help yourself or
anyone else. You must grow and learn by developing
and shaping your character to become a person others
will respect because of who you are. You also must
develop a competency in your area of passion and
purpose to complement your character development.

Who will *you* influence? Who will be drawn to you
and seek your advice, opinions, thoughts, and guidance?
Who will trust you? Who will buy-in? It will be those
most like you.

This is why you must realize the importance of your
character when it comes to attracting others. Think
about those close to you. Odds are you may not all be
working in the same profession or have the same
competency. However, you are likely to be similar in

terms of your level of character development.

We are attracted to others with character similar to ours or to those with a higher level of character development. People we aspire to be like.

You can imagine that common criminals do not hang around regularly with honest law abiding citizens. Neither is attracted to the other. Their character is as different as night and day.

Nor will you see those wasting their time and their lives associating frequently with very driven, focused, and productive people. These people are never attracted to each other. They are worlds apart in terms of their character development and worlds apart in terms of their accomplishments.

Habitual liars don't hang around honest people with high integrity. They simply are not attracted to one another.

These few examples should provoke some thought about character. Why do we attract others? Why are we attracted to others? The answer to both questions reveals much about who we are.

This is why character development is important. If you want to achieve high level results in your career, you must attract and influence others achieving high level results.

Our challenge is to grow our character in order to make a high impact within society. Once we have attracted others wanting to learn from us, how do we help them grow and learn? Three methods you can use to help another person grow are: teaching, mentoring, and coaching.

TEACHING

Merriam-Webster's definition of teaching:
- to cause or help someone to learn about a subject by giving lessons
- to give lessons about a particular subject to a person or group
- to cause or help a person learn how to do something by giving lessons, showing how it is done, etc.

"To 'teach' means to show. Teachers don't just tell; they illustrate, they model, they show." ~ Kevin Hall

Telling, illustrating, modeling, and showing are different ways of teaching someone what we know. Modeling has the greatest impact by far. We must live what we teach.

When we are teaching, we are simply transferring the knowledge we have to another person. This is where reading can play a big role. We cannot give what we do not have. In order to give knowledge, we must first possess knowledge. Teaching is typically one-way communication and is the least effective of the three methods. It's also the most common method.

Stop and Think: When someone has more knowledge than you, does this build trust or create distrust? Do they have more or less influence?

How does character come in to play with teaching? Reflect back to high school or college. Remember when more than one teacher taught the exact same subject from the exact same book? Most often, there was one teacher everyone wanted and recommended, and then there were the rest. Students were lucky to get the recommended teacher. What was different about the one compared to the rest? It was their character which determined their style. Who they were. When given a choice, character typically attracts us first while competency comes in second, if at all.

MENTORING:

Merriam-Webster's definition of mentor:
- someone who teaches or gives help and advice to a less experienced and often younger person

When we are mentoring, we are sharing experiences. Experiences cannot be transferred, only shared.

I always like to use the Grand Canyon as an example. If you have ever been there, you will understand this principle instantly. You cannot transfer the experience of being on the rim of the Grand Canyon. You can only share about what you saw and felt while you were there.

But, the only way to truly understand the magnificence of the Grand Canyon is to go there. There is no substitute. You must experience it in person. When you tell someone of an experience like this, you cannot transfer it. You simply share it knowing they would have to be there to truly understand.

You can transfer knowledge, and others can choose to accept it, apply it, and gain value from it as you have. Experiences are different. When we are mentoring, we are simply sharing our experiences with others to help them relate, to help them see more clearly, and to help them understand more deeply. We are attempting to paint a picture in their mind's eye.

COACHING

I define coaching as:
- helping others find their own answers from within

When we coach, we help people find their answers from within. We ask thought provoking questions causing them to pause, reflect, and go within to find their own answers. Our answer can never be as good for them as their own answer will be.

"If you fail to go within, you will go without."
~ Christian Simpson

No one can possibly know all of the variables you have experienced or are experiencing. No one knows you better than you. It's the same for others. They know themselves best. If we want to truly coach, we must learn to ask thought provoking questions moving others closer to their own answers.

When you are coaching others and asking them additional questions based on their answers to previous questions, it's important to remember this. Never ask them, *"Can you...?"* Asking someone *"Can you...?"* leads them to believe you doubt their abilities which leads them to question their own abilities as well.

Instead, ask them, *"How can you...?"* By adding the word *how*, you are implying there is a way. You believe it can be done. You have confidence in them. They simply must figure out *how*. This builds confidence and challenges them to begin to search for a solution.

These are three methods of influencing growth: teaching, mentoring, and coaching. Once someone has accepted your influence, it is time to do the influencing. It is no longer just about you. When you begin influencing others, assuming you have developed your character to a higher level, you need to accept the responsibility for helping them unleash more of their potential. Not only has your responsibility for yourself increased, your responsibility to others has increased.

When you start your leadership journey, it's about you leading you. It should be about you. You must do a lot of work to gain momentum. At the highest levels of leadership, it is no longer only about you. It's about what you can do to help others find and move along their path as they endure their journey. If you understand this, you understand influence.

My journey is bigger than me. It's about we. As a result of my growth, I am always trying to help others grow.

I would like to invite you to pause for a moment. In the spaces on the next page, write down the top five character traits you see in high impact leaders (people with significant influence) who are currently NOT attracted to you. Think of leaders you would like to attract in the future.

Note: If you're single and looking for Mr. or Mrs. Right, you can look at this exercise with a different perspective and consider the top five qualities you would like to see in a person you would like to attract to you for a personal relationship. List the top 5 character traits you would like them to have.

1. _____

2. _____

3. _____

4. _____

5. _____

Hopefully, you paused and took the time to think in depth about these five qualities. Do not cheat yourself in this area of learning. This matters, and it matters a lot.

Now, take a moment to reflect on the five people you associate with the most by choice. You may need a pen and paper. List and rate each of them on these same qualities using a scale of 1 to 10 with 10 being the highest.

It's important to slow down and spend time evaluating those closest to you. Not to blame or judge them, but to learn more about who you are by evaluating who they are.

Assuming you did the previous two exercises, now

honestly evaluate yourself on these same five qualities using the same 1 to 10 scale. Don't forget: who you are is who you attract.

Consider the top five people you spend the most time with. Why do you feel they are attracted to you? Your character is what attracts them. You are like them, and they are like you. If they are high impact leaders, great. If they are not, but you want to become a high impact leader, you won't get there without further development of your own character.

Note: If you looked at this exercise from a personal view point, consider who you hang around with and how they ranked. Consider how you ranked yourself. If you did not rank your friends and yourself high in these qualities, you will not attract a mate with the same qualities. You must first model them yourself.

As your influence increases, you will attract people with stronger character. Some will help you. Some will want your help. Your relationships will improve and strengthen as you begin to attract people with stronger character. These people have a common quality. They like to help others grow and get results. It's not about them. When it comes to people with strong character, you can always work with them for mutual benefit.

When we work with others, we benefit from the relationship of our minds working together on a common goal. What does this mean? None of us is as strong as all of us. None of us is as creative as all of us. None of us is as smart as all of us. The key principle is valuing the differences. If we do, we are always better together.

"Remember, when you have exhausted all possibilities, you haven't. There is always another way." ~ Thomas Jefferson

If you're not interested in working closely with others in order to use your influence to move them forward, you need to stop and consider this: you need people to help move you forward. If you are not helping others, you will not attract others willing to help you. You must be what you want those around you to be.

"The one who usually complains about the way the ball bounced is usually the one that dropped it." ~ Lou Holtz

If you are not attracting the right type of people to get you to where you want to go, there is only one reason. It's you. You may need people to hire you for a job or to have you provide a service. If you are not getting the right people to believe you can help them, you must figure out what about you needs to change and start making the necessary adjustments. If you want to change your results, you must change your mind.

If you cannot help the people you want to help, it's because you have not helped yourself enough. There are no shortcuts. You must pay the price and invest the time to achieve the results you desire. Too many people simply want what they want which results in them getting what they get which is not what they want. You must understand. You shouldn't simply go through change; you should intentionally grow through change.

When you are accepting change for no other reason than it is happening to you and you feel you have no control over it, you are being passive. However, when you become proactively involved in the change in your life, you quickly realize you have control. While others are living the lives they are given, you can choose to create the life you want. Instead of letting others decide your future, you can create your future.

For many of us, growing ourselves to a level where we are sought after by others for help requires us to travel far outside of our comfort zone. We may have to break old habits. It will be hard, but we can do it. To truly grow throughout life, we must learn, unlearn, and relearn constantly. Otherwise, we will remain stuck. No one wants to be stuck. Not me. Not you.

Stop and Think: Who can help you the most? Someone stuck in their comfort zone? Or, someone who consistently operates outside of their comfort zone where growth takes place? Who will have the most influence with the most people?

Think again about the people you want to attract. The people who can help you the most are not stuck. They are free to learn and grow. And, they are learning and growing. If you want to attract people who can help you move forward while you are helping them move forward, you must break free from your comfort zone and become comfortable being uncomfortable.

"The reason your comfort zone is comfortable is because you are not growing. You are acting by habit. It is easy and effortless. Comfort zone means you are settling for what you are today, and what you are today is all you'll ever be." ~ Paul Martinelli

You must make a habit of seeking discomfort. When you do, you will attract those same type of growth oriented people. If you want to attract people going someplace, you must be going someplace. If you want to attract people who are making things happen, you must be making things happen. That's how it works.

WHEN DO WE INFLUENCE?

14

WHEN DO WE INFLUENCE?

When there is a Desire, We Can Light Their Fire

"Life does not get better by chance. It gets better by change."
~ Jim Rohn

You cannot influence someone unless they want your influence. If they are happy where they are, they may not change. They may not feel there is a need to change. They may not have a desire to change and avoid those trying to influence them.

Merriam-Webster's definition of influence:
- the power to cause changes without directly forcing them to happen

Consider the five questions being addressed in this book:

1. Why do we influence?
2. How do we influence?
3. Where do we influence?
4. Who do we influence?
5. When do we influence?

The only question yet to be addressed is: When do we influence?

Regardless of how much you may want to influence someone, you will not influence them until they have a desire to change and want help.

When do *you* influence? You will only influence others when they want to be influenced by you. Just as you get to choose when others have influence with you, others have the same choice. They get to decide when they will accept or deny your influence.

It's possible to talk all day without influencing anyone. Talking to someone does not necessarily influence them. You have only influenced another person when they voluntarily change something they do because of something you said or something you did.

When you force someone to change, the other person has not really changed. They have only temporarily complied. Without the application of force and pressure, they will revert back to their old ways. Even with force and pressure, some still revert back when they get tired of complying. Too many people, especially with children young and old, force compliance and think they have succeeded in influencing and changing them.

They have not succeeded in changing them. They have simply achieved short term results through force, pressure, fear, coercion, and intimidation.

Stop and Think: Would you be more likely to seek help from someone who respects that you don't want their influence and simply supports you without pressure compared to someone attempting to relentlessly influence you when you don't want it? Which type of person would you trust the most?

If you force people to change, as a leader, you have no reason to be proud. Any person with weak character can force and intimidate others into compliance. The result is resentment not loyalty. If you tend to force and pressure others into compliance, you have a lot of character work to do before you can unleash your potential as a high impact leader.

Stop and Think: When someone tries to influence you when they know you don't want their influence, do they build trust or create distrust? Are you more likely or less likely to seek them out in the future?

In the past, you may have been frustrated with someone needing your help but not wanting your help. They didn't want to change. You wanted to help for the right reasons but were not allowed to help. We have all had those types of relationships. At some point, we have most likely also been the person unwilling to change when others wanted to help us. We were simply not ready and didn't have the desire to change.

Stop and Think: When do we accept someone's influence? When we want to change? Or, when we don't want to change?

We allow others to influence (lead) us only when we want and value their influence. Only when we want to change will we seek the influence of others. Reading this book is a perfect example. There is no way I can force my influence at this moment upon you. The only way I can influence you is if you choose to take action based on my words. It's your choice not mine.

You chose to begin reading this book. Then, you chose to continue reading it. Why? You're considering the influence I'm offering because we have a common interest: personal growth and leadership development. There is something you want to change about yourself.

In the end, you will decide whether or not I will influence you beyond these pages. Although my words have influenced you to read this book, I have not truly influenced you at a meaningful level unless you change something you do or become something you were not before because of the thoughts you developed while reading my words.

You only influence others *when* they want your influence, *when* they want your help, and ultimately *when* they want to change. I want to help you discover the value of change, positive change. Remember this, being unable to help someone you feel needs your help does not necessarily mean you are a low impact leader with low level influence. When someone isn't open to change, it doesn't make any difference who is in front of them. They are not going to be influenced.

Many people avoid change. They run from it. They hide from it. They ignore it. They hope *"it"* does not happen to them. You can be fully aware of the need for these people to change and not be able to influence them to change. You can be concerned about them but have no control or no influence over them.

Proactive people do not spend time focusing their attention in areas of concern where they have no control and no influence. Why would they? They have no control and no influence. It makes no sense to waste any time and energy in this area. People with weak character often spend a lifetime in their area of concern trying to change people who don't want to change.

You will know when you enter an area of concern. If you find yourself feeling frustrated, angry, mad, sad, upset, irritated, etc. because you have no control and no influence, you are in an area of concern. You have made a choice that is causing you to feel that way. You have chosen to enter an area where you have no control and no influence. Why would you stay there? You shouldn't.

You already know you have no control and no influence which causes you to begin to feel reactive and negative. That's the warning sign indicating you have entered an area of concern. You are operating outside your area of influence. You must maintain awareness relative to your influence.

If you have no influence, you are creating distrust as you try to forcefully influence others. You won't be motivating. You will be manipulating. There is no reason to remain in this situation. You are totally ineffective already because you have no control and no influence. It is simple to say. However, it is not so simple to do. You must be proactive, not reactive.

People often get caught up in areas of concern, and they dwell there for far too long. When this happens, their influence with others does not increase. It decreases. The effect is the exact opposite of what they're working toward if they're trying to increase their influence. Often, people choose to do it over and over and over again. They are being reactive instead of being proactive. They are responding based on their emotions instead of embracing the principles of influence.

Stop and Think: Do reactive people who are frustrated, mad, sad, angry, upset, irritated, etc. build trust with you or create distrust? When you're around them, does their influence increase or decrease?

Do not waste your time in areas of concern. Do not waste your time and energy trying to change someone who doesn't want to be changed. No matter how bad you may want to help them, they do not want it. When you continue to try and change them, you only push them farther away and decrease the chances of ever being able to help them. In this type of situation, your only option will be to offer support, not guidance.

There obviously are areas where you do have influence. This is where you want to invest your time. You will not suffer an onslaught of negative emotions when your focus is in your area of influence. Why? It's simple. You have control and influence in this area. You can make a difference. You will get positive results.

As you can imagine, proactive people invest their time and energy where they have control and influence. As a result, the area they have control and influence in grows much larger and eventually takes in territory that was previously in their area of concern. These people are filled with positive emotions. They are making a difference, a real and positive difference. They work patiently and persistently in their area of influence.

Working in your area of influence is simply a choice you must make many times each day. Ask yourself, *"Which area allows me to be most productive and most effective?"* An area where you have no control and no influence? Or, an area where you have control and influence? It's obvious while you are reading. However, when you want to change someone who needs to change but doesn't want to change, it's not so obvious.

You must become consciously aware when you leave your area of influence and enter your area of concern. There is only one person responsible for keeping you in your area of influence. You. It is not easy, but it is worth it in the long run. Your influence grows significantly when you develop the discipline to operate only where you have control and influence.

Which area do you think the people seeking your influence and help will be in? Your area of influence. These people will accept your influence. All others are outside your area of influence and inside your area of concern and will reject your influence. You do not forget about them. You acknowledge them, but you do not focus on them.

Have you ever thought about why people do not like change? Change makes people uncomfortable, and people naturally seek comfort over discomfort. There is something special about people who are constantly growing and stretching themselves. They have become comfortable being uncomfortable.

To continuously grow and unleash your potential, you also must become comfortable being uncomfortable. If you apply this basic principle of growth, your life will change profoundly. Make this mental note: You will only be able to influence and help those seeking discomfort and change.

Most people seek comfort unless they are high impact people who have become comfortable being uncomfortable. Many young people cannot wait to finish high school because they are uncomfortable learning and growing. Some do not finish because of their discomfort. They quit and never graduate. They give up. Relative to growth, they pay the price of living a life of comfort seeking while avoiding discomfort. Their only way forward is to choose discomfort and change in order to grow. If not, they will remain stuck.

Others excel through high school. They finish high school and cannot wait to get started with college. Just like high school, some don't make it. The discomfort of growth is too much to take. They give up. They quit college and must pay the price of living a life based on their choice to avoid the discomfort.

Again, some excel and graduate. Others continue on and receive graduate degrees. They have become more comfortable being uncomfortable. But eventually, they complete their formal education and are happy to be finished. At this point, many of them seek comfort.

They want to get the job their hard work has prepared them for. They want to settle in, earn a good income, and live their life. Too many people settle for this life. They finish their formal education and seek comfort. Although they have their entire careers to continue to intentionally grow, they don't. They get comfortable and rest on what they have done in the past.

The only discomfort they encounter is learning their new job. Occasionally, as they work their way along their professional career path, they may get promoted or change organizations which can potentially come with a little discomfort and growth, but it quickly ends. All they must do is become comfortable with the move and the new job or both, and they become comfortable again.

You may have noticed the more discomfort someone is willing to endure the more they will grow and unleash their potential. Unfortunately, many people count on what they have done in the past to get them to where they want to go in the future. If you want to be more, you must become more. What you have done so far is what got you to where you are. You must do more if you want to go farther. You must continue to stretch and grow yourself regardless of whether you are comfortable or not.

Being smart doesn't automatically cause you to turn your dream into your reality. You must also be dedicated. Will you make it happen? Are you willing to become comfortable being uncomfortable? If so, get ready. You are in for a career and a life that you likely cannot imagine at this point.

Too often, people are simply afraid to fail. When we try something new and are not successful, we typically learn from the experience. However, many people incorrectly say they failed. It's not failing unless you quit. If you keep trying, reflect on the experience, learn the lesson, and improve, it is simply a learning process. You are not failing when you don't succeed on the first try. You are learning how to succeed.

People with too much pride and ego seldom try anything new unless they have to. They are afraid of failing or learning in front of others. Therefore, they do not get as many opportunities to learn and grow. You must take responsibility for your own growth. If you are going to grow, you must learn something new.

"If we understand how we can change our mind, then we can change our life." ~ Bruce Lipton

The 4 Levels of Responsibility

As you read through these levels of responsibility, understand you are not always at the same level with everything in your life. You can be at different levels in different areas of your life at the same time.

For instance, you may be at Level 4 financially while you're at Level 1 relative to a relationship with someone in your life while you're at Level 3 on your new job while you're at Level 2 relative to your personal growth and development.

Level 1: Transferring Responsibility (no growth)

At Level 1, you are very comfortable. Some refer to this level as unconscious-incompetence. You don't know what you don't know. You are transferring responsibility for your life to others, and you don't know it. Your awareness of your ability to grow and accept responsibility is low. You don't know you should be growing and accepting responsibility for your future. You're not aware of what you're missing out on. You're coasting through life on what you or others have done in the past to get you to where you are today. You accept the life you have instead of choosing to create the life you want.

While you are at Level 1, you may be very uncomfortable externally with your life. You may be unhappy with your job, your income, your car, your home, your spouse, your children, your circumstances, and your life in general, but you are very comfortable with transferring the responsibility of improving it all to others. You do a lot of blaming and a lot of looking through the window at others instead of looking in the mirror at yourself.

You do this consciously and unconsciously. Either way, you are comfortable. You are only comfortable because you do not truly understand you're responsible. If you understood, things would be much different. But, you would no longer be at Level 1. You would be more advanced in your awareness and thinking.

Stop and Think: Do people transferring responsibility for their circumstances build trust or create distrust? Do they have more or less influence?

Level 2: Acknowledging Responsibility (no growth)

At Level 2, you are still comfortable. But, you are on the edge of your comfort zone. You know what you don't know. Some refer to this level as conscious-incompetence. You are acknowledging you can and should accept responsibility for your life, but you haven't actually done it. Your awareness is increasing. You know you should be growing and doing more. You have an awareness of what you are missing out on by continuing to transfer responsibility for your life to others. You are considering the things you can do to change what you don't like about your life. You are developing the desire to make changes and developing the vision of what life would be like if you took action.

While you're at Level 2, you may be uncomfortable externally with your life. You may be unhappy with your job, your income, your car, your home, your spouse, your children, your circumstances, and your life in general, and you're beginning to acknowledge your responsibility for improving it all. You're beginning to shift the focus of blame to yourself. Instead of looking through the window and blaming others, you start looking in the mirror and acknowledging responsibility.

You are consciously making the shift and considering you're actually responsible. However, you remain on the edge of your comfort zone because you haven't fully accepted responsibility. When you do, you will move to Level 3.

Stop and Think: Do people who acknowledge responsibility without fully accepting responsibility build trust or create distrust? Do they have more or less influence?

Level 3: Accepting Responsibility (growth happens)

At Level 3, you become uncomfortable. You're doing what you know you should be doing. Some refer to this level as conscious-competence. You are accepting responsibility for your life. You are choosing when and where you need to grow in order to be able to move yourself in the right direction. You have a higher level of awareness, and you know are responsible for every aspect of your life. You are consciously creating the life you want instead of continuing to accept the one you've been living. You are making changes while creating the vision for your future.

While you are at Level 3, you may still be uncomfortable externally with your life. You may still be unhappy with your job, your income, your car, your home, your spouse, your children, your circumstances, and your life in general, but you are doing something to improve it all. You are making progress and becoming more and more comfortable externally as you become uncomfortable internally as you accept more and more responsibility. You only blame yourself for what is wrong in your life.

You know you're responsible for your life. You became uncomfortable when you accepted the full burden of responsibility, and you're okay with it. You can no longer rest in comfort as your life passes you by. You must remain engaged learning, growing, and doing to align your life with your vision for your life.

"You can either accept reality as it is or create it as you wish it to be." ~ Michael Hyatt

Level 3 is where all growth happens. The key for sustained growth throughout your entire life is to become comfortable being uncomfortable. You must take responsibility for what you want to change in your life. When you're not focusing your energy and time on Level 3, you know you're letting others control your destiny.

Stop and Think: Do people accepting responsibility for themselves and their circumstances build trust or create distrust? Do they have more or less influence?

Level 4: Mastering Responsibility (no growth)

At Level 4, you are comfortable once again. You don't know what you know. Some refer to this level as unconscious-competence. You have made being responsible for those changes you made in your life at Level 3 a habit in your life at Level 4. You take full responsibility for continuing to do those things without consciously thinking about what you're doing.

While at Level 4, you are comfortable internally and externally with the aspects of your life that you have successfully addressed at Level 3. In these areas, there are no more problems. You have resolved these issues and moved on to tackle others. There is no blame here, only consistent and effective responsibility.

You are unconsciously doing things to demonstrate you are responsible for your life in these areas. You are comfortable because you are working on these things out of habit using your subconscious mind. You have mastered the areas of your life that you addressed effectively at Level 3. You have confidence in yourself and continuously climb through the levels in other areas of your life as you address other issues and seek additional growth.

What causes people to change and accept responsibility for their lives? Too often, it's the pain of hitting bottom. They have to. Other times, it's when they have seen enough, learned enough, or experienced enough that they develop a desire to make a change.

What foundation supports real change? What must you do in order to truly begin to initiate positive change in your life once you have accepted responsibility? How do you get started? What will determine if you are able to apply leadership principles and get real results?

I can tell you because I have done it, and I have read and heard many stories of others have done it. There is a commonality among people who have created a life of significance through constant change. They have made and continue to make tremendous sacrifices during their journey. In other words, they are willing to pay the price.

WILL YOU PAY THE PRICE?

15

WE MUST PAY THE PRICE

We Can't Go Up Until We Pay Up

"The price of anything is the amount of life you exchange for it."
~ Henry David Thoreau

Anything of value comes with a price. If you want to change your life, if you want to better apply something you have learned in this book, if you want to truly become a person with greater influence, you must be willing to pay the price. You must sacrifice. When you are through paying the price, you are through increasing your influence.

Some prefer the word investment over sacrifice. But, these are two very different words with two very different meanings. You must sacrifice in order to make the investment.

When we spend our time and money with expectations of a greater return in the future, we are making an investment. However, we must acknowledge the sacrifice that allowed the investment to be made. These are two distinctly different components of growth.

When you invest, you do not give up anything. You still have it. You may not have use of it, but you still possess it. You are placing something of value into a system and believe the system will increase the value of the investment over time. You believe the odds are in your favor. You believe you will recover the original investment plus an additional return in the future.

Sacrificing is something totally different than investing. When you sacrifice something, it is gone. It is not invested.

"When you make a sacrifice, you are giving up something of value today for something of greater value tomorrow."
~ John C. Maxwell

In 2006 after many years of dreaming about owning a Corvette, I purchased my dream car, a 2003 50th Anniversary Corvette Z06. It may not mean anything to you, but it meant a lot to me. I had never driven one before I purchased it. Life was good.

Fast forward to March 2011. I was starting to focus more on developing my character and was having thoughts of transforming my business from a Lean Manufacturing Consulting firm into a Professional Leadership Development firm.

It decided it was time for a sacrifice in an effort to prepare for my next phase of focused, intentional growth. I had several *"toys"* at the time and chose to sacrifice my dream car. I sacrificed my Corvette. It was not invested. It was given up.

This is an example of one of the many sacrifices I made while taking responsibility for my intentional growth. As I started to value new things at a higher level, I seemed to struggle less when giving up those things I had valued in the past. They seemed to naturally begin to fall away as my core values began to change.

This doesn't mean I will never have the things I want. But, when not having the things I want will move me in the right direction, I will take that option every time. My growth is now primary. Material possessions are now secondary.

What if you are not where you want to be? Many people are not where they want to be. I am still not where I want to be. Don't worry. It's possible for all of us to improve. Your life can always be better no matter how good or bad it is today.

"Though no one can go back and make a brand new start, anyone can start from now and make a brand new ending."
~ Carl Bard

You can improve. I can improve. We all can improve. *IF*, we will sacrifice. And *IF*, we are willing to pay the price.

I am going to share a few more sacrifices from my life. Mentoring is the best way to help you better understand sacrifice. I'll tell you about my sacrifices and why I made them. Most importantly, I'll share what I expected to change after making them. Some were sacrifices that helped develop my character. Some were sacrifices that helped develop my competency. Remember, 87% of our results come from our character (who we are) and 13% come from our competency (what we know).

There have been many sacrifices along the way. I'm sure there will be many more in my future. As I started making intentional sacrifices, I slowly began to understand there would be rewards as I moved forward if I made the right choices. Choices that would allow me to leverage the sacrifices for my benefit.

Either directly or indirectly, all of our sacrifices are related to our growth. But, we must do more than sacrifice. After making the necessary sacrifices, we must do the hard work of applying ourselves in the area in which we want to grow and improve.

I did not make many significant sacrifices on the front end of my career between 1988 and 1995. I was not sacrificing, and I was not growing intentionally. My growth was purely on-the-job *"accidental"* growth during those years. I only grew because I was bored and wanted to learn more about the equipment and processes as I performed the highly repetitive daily tasks of a front line, entry-level factory worker operating a machine in a manufacturing facility.

Things changed in 1995 when I started making intentional sacrifices. While working full-time with lots of daily and weekend overtime, I enrolled in college as a single parent. Eric meant the world to me then as he still does today. He was only four years old at the time.

He had no idea he was influencing my decisions. I wanted to spend more time with him and provide a better life for him. I was familiar with sacrificing to earn more, but I wasn't familiar with sacrificing to learn more.

That was something new for me, but I was ready for a change. I wanted to be more, so I could do more while hoping that I would have more. I wasn't familiar with any principles of leadership at that time. I was in the trial and error phase of life, but I was learning how to intentionally develop myself. Knowing what I know now about *The 4 Levels of Responsibility*, I was beginning to do some work at Level 3: Accepting Responsibility.

I wanted to spend more time with Eric in the future. However, I knew I would have to spend less time with him on the front end in order to study and go to classes for the next six or seven years as I worked to earn my college degree.

I remember thinking, *"Eric will be 10 or 11 when I*

finish college. I will miss a lot of time with him in the coming years. But, I would rather miss six or seven years instead of missing all of them because I was still working evenings, night shifts, and seven days a week for the rest of my career on the front lines as an hourly factory worker."

I knew I would have to sacrifice much of my personal life. I would have preferred to be hunting, fishing, or working overtime to earn extra money instead of going to classes and studying. I was barely making ends meet financially. Although I was grateful my company was reimbursing me for tuition and books, I still had to pay in advance, pay for fuel to get to and from classes, and purchase a computer and a printer along with other supplies. More and more sacrifice. But, it was all worth it.

"You must give up to go up!" ~ *John C. Maxwell*

You not only must give up to go up. You must give up more to stay up once you get there. Then, if you want to continue to go farther up, you must give up even more. Sacrifice never ends when you're constantly and intentionally growing. Fortunately, the rewards also never end.

If I had never made all of those sacrifices, I would still be doing the same basic entry-level, factory jobs. When you sacrifice long enough and often enough, you begin to positively impact not only your life, but also the lives of others. Some will be close to you. Others you may never know, but you will make a greater and more positive impact in the world if you learn and apply the principles related to sacrifice.

After finally graduating from college several years later in December 2002, I immediately sacrificed my job security in February 2003. At the time, I had been at the same organization for 14 years. I had tons of experience and could do nearly any job in the facility relative to operations and production.

However, I had also learned the value of sacrifice. So after graduating, I chose to continue sacrificing by giving up the security I had worked so hard to establish and accepted a job offer at a different company.

I was through with college, and I had no plans to continue my formal education. My days of sacrificing were over, right? Not at all, although I did slow down for a few years until I realized the growth opportunities associated with the college degree were over. I had to make a decision: maintain the status quo or find a way to continue to grow.

I wanted to keep growing. In 2005, I became inspired to start reading books on Lean Manufacturing after we had a Lean Consultant come into our facility to lead a Lean (kaizen) event for a week. After watching him in action, I said to myself without a doubt, *"I can do what he's doing! I can be a Lean Manufacturing Consultant, and I would love to do it."* I love change, and I love process improvement. So, Lean Manufacturing (process improvement) was a natural fit, and I quickly developed a passion for it.

I committed to start reading, learning, and applying. Over and over and over, book after book. I read a lot. I sacrificed much of my personal time reading Lean books for the next three years. I became a Lean expert in the eyes of others simply by reading and applying what I was learning. I still have much to learn and always will have much to learn because we never arrive. When it comes to learning, there is no finish line.

Using the Lean Manufacturing principles I had

learned, I led the Lean transformation of our entire facility. We transformed from a traditional batch & queue operation into a streamlined single-piece flow operation in only three short years. We achieved amazing results by anyone's standards as we improved from -3% GPM (gross profit margin) to +35% GPM.

We added approximately 50 new jobs without having to hire a single new person. We had freed up people internally because of the improvements we had made. We also freed up 70,000 ft^2 of a 150,000 ft^2 facility during the transformation which allowed us to add new equipment related to new departments without building on to the existing facility. We reduced employee turnover significantly. We started saving millions of dollars annually. We also had a lot of fun.

In 2008, after three years of consistent results and more tremendous growth and learning, it was time for my biggest sacrifice yet. It was time to sacrifice my entire income. The income and security I had worked 20 years to obtain.

I chose to give it all up. One day, I was secure and earning an annual salary I never imagined I would be earning. The next day, I had voluntarily given it all up. I was earning zero income and had no benefits. I had decided to start my own Lean Manufacturing Consulting business from scratch. I wanted to follow my passion and make a bigger impact across multiple organizations.

Many people often say to me, *"I wish I had my own business."* My reply is, *"Do you want to make the sacrifices needed to start and create your own business?"* Many people want the end result, but they don't want to pay the price required along the way in order to get the results they want. They want what they want without having to give up what they've got to get it.

It wasn't easy to do what I did. Sacrifice it all. Sacrifice my job. Sacrifice my income. Sacrifice my retirement savings. But, sacrificing has been *"working for me."* In this context, I define *"working for me"* as moving me in the right direction closer to my goal. Many will *"wish for what they want,"* but few are willing to *"sacrifice to get what they want."*

I have met many people, better off financially than I was at the time, who have the ability and potential to do very well if they would simply step out and start their own business. Most often however, they are not willing to make the required sacrifices to actually do it. They may not believe in themselves. Maybe, they haven't developed themselves. They may be afraid to bet on themselves. If they won't bet on themselves, why should anyone else?

When I talk to them, some say, *"I would give anything to have my own business."* I usually reply with these questions. Will you give up your toys? Will you give up your security? Will you give up your nice cars, your nice home, your retirement nest egg, your 9 to 5 routine? Will you give up your weekends playing, golfing, hunting, fishing, partying, or whatever it is you like to do with your free time?

If necessary, are you willing to give it all up? Not forever, but until you can create the life you want. If not, odds are you will never get to live that life. No one on this planet is interested in creating the life you want for yourself except you.

There is a big difference in saying and doing. Many people want to talk about doing something, but few want to actually do something. Sacrifice is not easy. It's hard. We feel the loss instantly. The reward may not be felt for months or even years.

It is interesting to me how many talented people choose to give up a life of significance for a life of security. We did not bring anything with us into this life, and we are not taking anything with us when our life is over. Why are we worried about hanging on to every little thing we ever acquire? Those things are anchors cast by us. They are holding us back and keeping us from reaching our full potential.

As I started my business, Ria and I had to give up many of the things we had taken for granted. We had to stop dining out. We had to be selective about where and when we spent money. It took me nearly eight months to get established and begin to earn a steady income again.

As it had been in the past, all of the sacrifices had been worth it. I was making a bigger impact across multiple organizations. I was developing others to do what I was doing. My income was much greater. I was much happier. Win-win! Everything was better. I had made the right decision, against the odds of the Great Recession of 2008-2009, when I gave up the best job I ever had while many others were losing their jobs.

During the eight month time period I was building my business, I spent much of my time driving to meetings with potential clients. It was during that time in the fall of 2008 when I was exposed to professional leadership for the first time. That was when I first discovered *The 7 Habits of Highly Effective People*.

I started learning much more about the principles I had already been applying. But more importantly, I started to learn about many I hadn't even considered.

I didn't know it at the time. But, I was about to begin transforming myself from the inside out. The sacrifices were about to get more personal. I learned my focus needed to be on me and my interactions with others. I discovered there was much opportunity for me to grow and get better as a person. I had come a long way with my competency, but I had a long way to go with my character. That was when my formal, on purpose for a purpose, leadership journey started. Personal sacrifices became much greater. I immediately started sharing my new knowledge with everyone I interacted with personally and professionally. I did it intentionally for two reasons.

First of all, I wanted them to learn what I was learning and be able to improve their lives by learning to apply it in their lives. I wanted to expose them to key leadership principles they may not have thought about in the past.

Secondly, I realized sharing what I was learning with others would cause me to hold myself accountable at a higher level. They would know how I was supposed to be living my life and how I should be leading myself and others. I was establishing accountability to others.

As I taught and trained people about Lean Manufacturing while leading Lean improvement events and conducting Lean Certification courses, I began to start teaching leadership principles in all of my events and sessions. I had a desire to make a positive difference in the lives of others as well as to improve my own life. I quickly developed a passion for sharing what I was learning.

The sacrifices relating to my exposure to leadership in 2008 had been the amount of time spent reading, learning, and applying what I discovered in leadership books and audios. I was once again sacrificing my time regularly and consistently to grow myself as I started doing when I enrolled in college in 1995. But this time, it was different. This time I was learning my character needed attention. Previously, I had been doing what many people do. I had been focused on developing my competency or my knowledge.

In 2008, it was time to begin my personal transformation. I started my leadership journey with a heavy focus on acquiring knowledge. I did increase my knowledge about leadership principles between 2008 and 2012. As I did, the most important thing I learned was that my character mattered more than my competency.

Humble people learn from their mistakes. If you are truly humble, you cannot be humiliated. However, ego-driven and prideful people are humiliated by their mistakes. The humble person has a teachable spirit and grows while the ego-driven, prideful person believes they already know it all and slows.

When it comes to character, if you wouldn't want what you are about to do to be blasted out on all of your social media platforms, you shouldn't do it. For instance, consider these examples: what you are about to say, how you are about to say it, what you just said, what song you are about to listen to, what TV show or movie you are about to watch, what words you are about to use, how you are about to treat your loved ones, what joke you are about to tell, how you are about to spend your time, and what you are about to do behind someone's back.

We should strive to align our character with what's right. Not only when someone is looking, but when no one is looking. Who we are all the time determines the total amount of influence we will have and how many people we will be able to influence.

I've made many mistakes. I will make many more mistakes, but what's most important is that I learn from my mistakes. I'm nowhere close to perfect, but I am intentionally improving. I have successfully transformed my life. I'm proud to be much better today than I had ever been in the past.

I am far from finished. I have much more work to do as I continue to apply leadership principles to climb to the next level of influence and beyond. We should never stop working on ourselves. The job of improving ourselves will never be complete.

We should have a vision and a mission for our lives. Every choice we make should build trust with others. We cannot go where we want to go alone. We need others to help us. Everything we do and everything we are matters. The greater we want our influence to be, the greater we must be.

Stop and Think: If you demonstrate the discipline to make good decisions about your life, will you build trust or create distrust? Will your influence increase or decrease?

Early on, I spent some time in the U. S. Marine Corps Reserves as an infantryman and a lot of time on the front lines in manufacturing organizations. One thing common to both is the endless use of profanity. Believe me, I did my share. Using profanity was a habit of mine from my early teenage years until I was in my early 40s in 2012 when I stopped completely. I don't do it anymore. If you're around me publicly or privately, you won't ever hear a single word of profanity.

I don't judge others, but I do look in the mirror and

work on what I can, ME! Every small win is really a huge victory when it comes to developing our character.

I made a choice to start communicating without profanity, no matter where I am or who I'm talking to. In the past, I thought it would never be possible. Years later, I no longer must catch myself even thinking of those words when I'm speaking. They have been removed from my vocabulary.

This was another small example of my giving up to grow up. It was another small way to increase my influence with the right people by doing the right thing and becoming the right person. It was about continuing to develop my character.

I started making significant financial sacrifices when I went to John Maxwell's *A Day About Books* event in 2012. I started investing in myself and my family. I always ask myself, *"Will what I am about to spend this money on move me in the right direction?"* If the answer is yes, I should spend it. It's an investment in my future. If the answer is no, I shouldn't spend it. It's a waste of time and money.

I, Ria, Eric, and my Mom became John Maxwell Certified Speakers, Trainers, and Coaches in 2012-2013. Ria, Eric, and I also enrolled in the John Maxwell Mentorship program. Ria and I invested many thousands of dollars and many thousands of hours developing ourselves using these and other programs.

However, the John Maxwell Certification and Mentorship Program weren't intended to be the end for us. They were simply additional stepping stones along our leadership path as Ria and I continued to grow and develop our own leadership development brand.

These programs raised my awareness because I was

not only representing myself, but also John Maxwell during that time. This awareness led me to make additional choices to further strengthen my character and increase my influence with other high impact leaders.

We have participated in multiple training sessions with John Maxwell, Les Brown, Nick Vujicic, and attended many other leadership seminars featuring other leadership professionals. We sacrificed absolutely everything we could financially to develop and grow ourselves, our family members, and our leadership development business. If we won't invest in ourselves, why should anyone else? If they won't and we don't, how can we expect to improve?

Many people would never consider sacrificing their retirement money, their favorite toys (cars, boats, motorcycles, ATV's, personal water craft), vacations, etc. and tons of time and money in order to grow themselves personally. However, we must sacrifice to truly move forward.

What are you willing to do to get from where you are to where you want to be? What do you need to sacrifice?

Growth doesn't just happen. You must make it happen by becoming intentional and focused on creating your preferred future.

It's easy for you to separate yourself from average people getting average results if you want to make exceptional choices to achieve exceptional results. It's not a matter of *"Can you do it?"* It's a matter of *"Will you do it?"* You can become exceptional, and you should.

MY PERSONAL JOURNEY FROM THERE TO HERE

16

CREATING THE LIFE I WANT

When I Became Intentional, Things Changed

"It is in your moments of decision that your destiny is shaped."
~ Tony Robbins

In these final few chapters in an effort to give real meaning to the leadership principles I've shared with you, I'll share some personal stories of how I have applied the principles in this book to my life. In this chapter, I describe how I started my intentional growth journey. In the next chapter, I reveal how I discovered my passion. Then, I'll share a chapter explaining how I followed my passion to find my purpose.

As I took responsibility for leading myself, the biggest obstacle I had to overcome along the way was ME! It's the same for everyone. The biggest obstacle between where we are and where we want to be is always self. It always has been. It always will be.

In 1995, I was a reactive, short tempered, entry level, front line, factory worker with no college education and no desire to have one. Today, nearly 20 years later in 2014, I'm writing my first book on leadership and will be writing many more in the coming years. What changed? My mind. My thinking. And, my awareness.

Leadership is about adding value to yourself in order to add value to others which positions you to become valued by others.

I had to value myself before anyone else could, would, or should. It started with me working on me. It is still about me working on me. It will always be about me working on me because I've noticed I have been involved with every problem I've ever had.

Has my transformational journey been easy? NO WAY! Has it been worth it? ABSOLUTELY!! Will it ever end? There is no finish line. Can you grow to a higher level? SURE YOU CAN! Will you do it? Only you know the answer. However, I hope to inspire you to do it.

I remember having the big *"AHA!"* moment you often hear people speak of when they talk about turning their lives around. I'm referring to the moment I decided to truly begin leading (influencing) myself positively in order to change the direction of my life. I decided to write a new script for my life instead of continuing to live the script I had accepted. I was about to start working on myself for myself.

This decision had a big impact on my life. I had no idea it would be the beginning of a never-ending growth journey and a story of personal leadership. At the time, I thought if you were a leader that meant you were a boss. Like everyone else, I knew there were good bosses and not so good bosses. That was the extent of my understanding of leadership.

The year was 1995, and I was 25 years old. I was working in Auburn, Alabama. It was around 2 am. I had on old, dirty jeans, an old t-shirt, greasy steel-toed boots, safety glasses, and an old, dirty blue jean apron hung around my neck as I tried to stay clean. As usual, I was at work in the middle of the night when most people were home sleeping soundly with their families.

I operated a large drill press and a CNC lathe machining holes into steel parts. It was a dirty, boring job, but it paid the bills. I was in the middle of what would become a three month streak of working 12 plus hours a day for seven days a week without a day off. It was nothing new. I had been doing factory work nearly seven years since I initially started working in a production machine shop in 1988. Long hours and weekend work were a normal part of my life.

On that particular night, there was a corporate industrial engineer from our headquarters observing me. He was there to do what is called a time observation study. I was surprised. He could have done what he had to do on the day shift. I wondered, *"Why is he here in the middle of the night? With me?"*

Shortly after arriving, he told me Don Large Sr., the Plant Manager, had asked him to work with me because I consistently recorded high production. I had always seen productivity as a form of competition. To add a component of fun to the job, I loved the challenge of finding a better or faster way to perform the tasks. Continuous improvement was a hobby for me while at work and broke up the monotony of the long hours.

As I worked, the engineer observed me. He used a stopwatch to capture my time performing various steps of the operation. After we got to know each other, he began to tell me about a conversation he had with Don about me. He said Don believed I had the potential to become more than *"just a machine operator"* if I would apply myself and get additional education.

The new visitor had no idea I had barely graduated high school because I did not make an attempt to apply myself. I regularly made the following comments. I will never go to college. I hated school. My goal was to graduate high school. I did. I'm done.

Hearing about the comment Don made was surprising because I wasn't a stellar employee during my first few years working in his plant.

I had joined the U.S. Marine Reserves in 1987 as an infantryman. I chose the infantry although my test scores would have allowed me to do something much different. I graduated from boot camp at Parris Island, South Carolina in December 1987 and went straight to infantry school at Camp Geiger, North Carolina, graduating in February 1988.

I was reactive and short tempered before I went through Marine training. I was much worse afterward. I would easily get angry over little things in just a few seconds. I was my biggest obstacle.

Luckily for me, I met Howard Hoyle in infantry school. When we returned home from our infantry training, he was able to help me get a job in a manufacturing plant in Montgomery, Alabama where his father was a supervisor. I worked there about a year before being laid off and making my way into Don Large Sr.'s plant in September 1989.

I was always very productive and got along with people for the most part as long as they left me alone. I was young and ignorant. I let people of all ages push my buttons. When they did, everyone saw the worst of my short temper. It was ugly, and I'm not proud of it. I didn't know what I didn't know. I had a lot to learn and a lot to unlearn.

I assumed my consistently high productivity was the only reason they had not fired me. The *"potential"* Don saw in me may have had something to do with it too. I could not see that potential at the time. Either way, if they had fired me, I would have deserved it without question. Fortunately, they never did. They gave me chance after chance along the way. For that, I am grateful.

I recently had the pleasure of visiting with Don. He is now 80, retired, full of energy, and doing great. He shared a story about a meeting he had with me while I was still struggling with self-control. At first, I didn't remember the meeting at all. Then, it started to come back to me as Don started sharing the details.

Don explained I had been involved in several issues as a front line employee early in my career under his leadership. At this point, it was time for him to take action. It was time for me to shape up or ship out. So, he requested a meeting with me and my supervisor.

As Don shared the story with me, he said he intended to be, and was, very hard on me in an effort to help me grow or go. He said he was very surprised and impressed by how polite I was during the meeting considering all he had heard about me and my short temper. Ultimately, he gave me a choice: resign or straighten up immediately. I said I would straighten up immediately. Don remarked, *"Well, get out there and get to work."* And, the meeting was over.

I did and instantly started to become a better employee. My integrity has always mattered. When I say I will do something, I do it. Don cared for me then and cares for me now. I could feel it then, and I could still feel it during our recent meeting. He's a great person.

One interesting thing Don mentioned to me during that recent visit was a call I made to him one year after the meeting. He said no one had made a call to him during his entire career like the one I made. I called him back exactly one year later on the anniversary of the meeting to thank him for giving me one last chance and believing in me when I didn't believe in myself. I called to confirm that he knew I had made the changes he requested and intended to continue to improve. Don was very impressed. He still seemed to be all these years later.

On my recent visit, he mentioned telling this story many times as the years passed, even as recently as a few weeks prior to my visit. He said my actions left an impression. He felt I grew over the years and was a great team member. Thanks for believing in me Don.

Let's return to the time observation study I mentioned earlier. Throughout that night, the total stranger expressed his belief in me and continued to do his best to get me to see my potential, the potential Don had expressed he saw in me. As the stranger encouraged me, I continued to reject anything he said about going to college.

I never expected to go to college. I knew who I was and what I wanted. I didn't need anyone else, especially a stranger from the corporate office in another state, telling me what I needed to do to advance in the company.

What did he know about me? Nothing I thought. But, he did know what Don knew, *"I had potential."* They knew it. I didn't.

The engineer's last name was Patel. I had never seen him before and never saw him again. I would love to share this book with him and thank him for his inspiration and his belief in me.

You may also never realize the difference you have made in the lives of others. He has no idea how his words impacted me. I didn't even know at the time. This is why it is important to always take the time to slow down and connect with someone when you see potential in them. They may not see the potential within themselves. Thank you Mr. Patel! You inspired me to intentionally rewrite my script and to change my life.

We shook hands when he left, and I thanked him for his words of support. I thought it was just another night in the grind of factory work. But, something had happened. I started thinking differently. Don's belief in me had planted a seed of possibility inside of me.

I began to ask myself many questions. What's possible? What if I went to college? What would change? Should I do it? Could I do it? How could I do it? When could I do it?

Shortly after my conversation with Mr. Patel, I decided to take immediate action and enrolled in Southern Union State Community College the very next semester. I had not only decided to rescript my life. I was officially doing it. I was about to make a major change.

"We already live with many scripts that have been handed to us, the process of writing our own script is actually more a process of 'rescripting,' or paradigm shifting – of changing some of the basic paradigms that we already have.

As we recognize the ineffective scripts, the incorrect or incomplete paradigms within us, we can proactively begin to rescript ourselves." ~ Stephen R. Covey

I started college, as a single parent, while working long hours and weekends to make ends meet. I didn't enjoy high school, so volunteering for more schooling was a big sacrifice.

In high school, I was focused on being funny, having fun, hanging out, and working to make money, so I could hang out more. Neither of my parents graduated high school. I barely graduated. But, graduating was a big deal, no matter my GPA. If it had been much lower, I would not have been eligible for a diploma. I didn't care. My results were a mirror image of my thoughts. Poor at best.

This time, it was my choice. I was choosing to go to college. Things were going to be different. I cared about my grades. I understood my grades mattered, and someone would be looking at them and judging me. I made an *"A"* in the first class. I was focused. I was on a mission, and it showed. I was getting results. With only a few exceptions, I made all A's from start to finish.

It took me nearly five years to get my two year degree, but I did it. I was paying the price to change my circumstances. I had potential, and I was validating it with my GPA. I did not want to be a machine operator 10, 20, 30, or worse, 40 years later. I was changing the way I thought and the way I lived my life. I was slowly beginning to transition away from being a reactive person and was becoming a proactive person.

After a year and a half break, I enrolled in an accelerated Executive Bachelor of Business Administration (BBA) program at Faulkner University in Montgomery, Alabama which allowed me to get my next two years of college in only one year. I was going to make up for lost time. Because I had already been enrolled in college for years, I was also growing within the organization, I had worked my way into a position which would allow me the opportunity to attend the required 42 Saturdays on the campus, which was an hour away, during the one year accelerated program.

I was beginning to value higher level things which allowed me to let go of lower level things. I didn't have to give them up. They simply fell away.

More sacrifice. I was at it again. I basically had to sacrifice everything for one year. I was either working, in class, doing homework, or studying for the next test. We had tests every week except the first week of each of the six modules making up the program. Again, I excelled.

I strongly believed in myself and my abilities at that point. I was on a mission. I made an *"A"* in every class that year except one. I graduated with highest honors. I had a poor attitude in high school and a great attitude in college. Different attitude. Different results!

"What lies behind us and what lies before us are tiny matters compared to what lies within us." ~ *Oliver Wendell Holmes*

I was beginning to understand this principle: We have infinite potential and are able to continually grow as long as we are living. When our formal education is over at any level whether high school or college, we must ask ourselves, *"Will we choose to grow?"* or *"Will we choose to slow?"* I was beginning to consistently choose growth.

Since 1995, I had been intentionally applying myself on the job too. I had worked my way up through various positions learning a lot along the way and became a setup person learning to changeover and setup most of the CNC machines in the entire facility. I later accepted a process technician position and was responsible for programming most of the CNC machines. Computerized drafting to create tooling, setup, and process drawings for the manufacturing processes were also my responsibilities. Then, I became a technical analyst issuing quotes for special products, consulting with engineers on the design of those products, and working with the manufacturing group to determine processing requirements and lead-times for the products.

Although I was not formally educated as an engineer, I qualified for this engineering position because of my many years of experience with the various manufacturing processes and people within the organization.

I graduated in December 2002 with my Executive BBA. After 14 years with a great organization, it was time to move on and continue my growth. I immediately put my degree to use and resigned to advance my career in February 2003 with another organization. That was simply the next natural step of my journey. With a large salary increase due to the many years of growth and sacrifice, payback came quickly. I had developed a strong passion for growing, learning, and changing.

17

DISCOVERING MY PASSION

My Lean Manufacturing Journey

"Ever since I was a child I have had this instinctive urge for expansion and growth. To me, the function and duty of a quality human being is the sincere and honest development of one's potential." ~ *Bruce Lee*

Almost immediately after graduating from college, I accepted a position as a cost estimation engineer at a company across town in early 2003. It was time for a change and more growth.

Little did I know, moving to a new organization would eventually lead me to meet someone a few years later with high level leadership skills, Jim Noreault.

I had never had the opportunity to report directly to someone like Jim in my career. I didn't know what I had been missing. I've since discovered people like Jim are rare. I hope you have or someday get to experience his style of leadership in action. It was amazing and inspiring.

Jim held the top formal position within the facility. Everyone ultimately reported to him, either directly or indirectly.

By the time Jim joined the company as the new Plant Manager, I had moved from cost estimation engineer to process engineer and had recently been selected to fill a newly created position, Lean Coordinator. Lean is a term commonly used in the manufacturing industry and is defined as a coordinated, common sense approach to identifying and eliminating waste in any process by working smarter not harder.

The Lean Coordinator position had not existed in the past because we had not been using the methods and techniques of continuous improvement related to Lean. This multi-billion dollar, global company was just beginning to formally embrace Lean. I would be responsible for leading the transformation within our facility with Jim's support.

Throughout my career, I had always been interested in process improvement and was excited about the Lean Coordinator position. I would be responsible for leading continuous improvement in the entire 150,000 ft² facility. I had to train, grow, and lead myself while I was simultaneously training, growing, and leading the entire team. We were all learning Lean together.

I remember the first time Jim walked into my office. He introduced himself, sat down on the edge of my desk, and asked me, *"What is your role here?"* I said, *"I'm the recently appointed Lean Coordinator."* He asked, *"Who do you report to?"* I said, *"You."* I loved his reply, *"Good, because if you didn't, you do now."* I will never forget him. I'm excited to get to share my admiration for Jim with you.

I thought to myself. Things are about to change. The new guy gets it. I had already been reading and studying Lean books. I knew reporting directly to the top was important to ensure an effective Lean transformation. I did not want to be tangled in another manager's personal agenda which is often a problem when the Lean leader does not report to the highest plant level leader.

Jim knew this too. He got it. We were about to make things happen. He was ready, and I was ready.

Jim was always in the middle of the real work. On one occasion, he asked the top managers to put on gloves and get involved with the people and the processes to learn what problems the people were experiencing. He had the front line operators train the managers to do the real work for a few hours while observing and discussing problems.

Leaders get in the middle of it, not to micromanage, but to learn from and connect with the people doing the work. Jim had his gloves on leading the way. He was on the team. It was awesome. Afterward, he asked me and the managers to meet him in the conference room.

Once we were there and the door was closed, Jim simply asked, *"What problems did you discover?"* He proceeded to write them all down on the white board as the managers provided feedback. Once the problems were listed on the board, he turned to us and smiled before saying, *"Now, go fix them."*

Then, he turned around and walked out of the room, closing the door on his way out. I LOVED IT then, and I LOVE IT even more today. I was learning what real leadership looked like, and I liked the way it looked. More importantly, I liked the way it felt. I have told this story many times throughout the years to different people and teams while conducting Lean and Leadership training.

When I reflect on Jim attacking those problems head on and the resistance we often got from others, I think of how often I hear people say, *"That's the way we've always done it. Why change it?"* This is common. Far too many people want to hang on to the old ways of doing things which not only costs them, but doing so also costs the organization they are supposed to be helping.

Jim liked developing new solutions for old problems. I did too. The traditional way of thinking is, *"If it ain't broke, don't fix it."* The Lean way of thinking is, *"Fix it, so it doesn't break."* We started fixing a lot of things that weren't broken.

Jim made it clear from the start. He was supporting Lean from the top, and I reported directly to him as the Lean Coordinator. He clarified I was there to support him and his team of managers. He also clarified what was expected from them by telling them, *"It is your job to transform your areas and this facility using Lean principles. If you don't know how or need help, that's why Mack is here. It is not Mack's job to do it by himself. It is your job to improve your area of operations. If you need help with Lean and Mack does not or cannot help you, let me know."*

I liked Jim's style of leadership.

Jim made me out to be the good guy. He was ensuring I would be successful during the Lean transformation. He also clearly identified himself as the target for those who were not onboard. He knew as the leader of change I would quickly be considered the bad guy by those resistant to change.

Jim gave me breathing room. I could do my job with his full support. I could be successful. This was his style. He was a leader of people, and he made things happen with people who wanted to make things happen.

My unofficial Lean journey had actually started many years before in 1995 while I was a machine operator. The company I was with transformed from batch & queue production (large lots of parts waiting in piles) to cellular manufacturing (single-piece, efficient flow). With Jim's support, I would become a highly effective transformational Lean leader.

I learned a lot. I bought in right away. I was naturally and continuously looking for ways to improve, I've always loved change, and I always will. Without change, there can be no improvement. This principle applies to people and processes. However, most people do not like change and struggle with the concept of continuous improvement.

This was much different from my first experience with Lean in 1995. It was 10 years later, and I was not just along for the ride this time. It was 2005, and I was going to be driving. I had never led a Lean transformation, but I was excited to make it happen. Without ever having received any formal Lean training, I simply held up my hand and said, *"I will take the responsibility, learn to do it, and learn to lead it."* I loved everything about Lean.

Jim allowed me to read Lean books at work. I also read them at home. I was passionate about Lean and didn't mind sacrificing my personal time to get better and to go faster. I was finally excited to be working in manufacturing. The catch was, I wasn't working any longer. I was having fun. I was getting paid to do what I loved to do. And, I was hooked.

I would read about Lean. Learn a new Lean principle. Experiment through application. Then, repeat. Over and over. Once I was comfortable with a set of principles, I would assemble a team and teach them what I had learned. Then, lead them through the application process of making improvements in the plant using the Lean principles. We quickly began to get tremendous results.

Jim was pleased. I was pleased. Everyone was pleased except those who were still resistant to change. But we did it, and we did it well. Lean principles are similar to leadership principles. They are common sense and easy to understand, but they are not commonly practiced. They say easy and do hard.

After achieving solid, verifiable successes repeatedly, Jim decided to create a Lean Manager position and promoted me to fill it. Jim was expanding his management team. Based on our local success, I was asked to travel to several of our other facilities in the U.S. and Mexico to support and help them with their Lean initiatives. We were making a difference, not only in our facility, but also throughout the organization. We had developed a lot of influence.

In early 2008, after several years of great success, Jim called me to his office one day to tell me the Quality Manager had resigned. He wanted me to take on the Quality Manager's responsibilities while continuing to serve as the Lean Manager. I appreciated his confidence in me. I had much respect for Jim but had also expressed to him previously that I wasn't interested in carrying out the duties of the Quality Manager. Not because I didn't value quality, but because it would put me behind a desk, on the phone, and take me away from what I loved, process improvement on the shop floor with the people.

However, I told Jim I would accept the Quality Manager role too if necessary. But, I couldn't promise how long I would do it because I didn't want to do it. After work, I thought about it and decided not to do it at all. I went in several hours early the next morning, started cleaning out my desk, and gathering my stuff. I was resigning without a notice.

I had found something I was passionate about. Lean Manufacturing. No one, not even Jim, was going to take me away from it. I fully understood his position. As the

Plant Manager, he was doing what was best for the plant and the organization. That was his job.

But, I was doing what was best for me and my future. That was my job because I had always understood I was getting paid by someone else, but I was always working for myself.

I respected Jim, but I was going to miss him.

I was truly continuing to intentionally lead myself toward the future I desired instead of accepting what I was given and dealing with it as I had effectively done over the past 20 years. Jim convinced me to give him 30 days in order to *"give it a try."*

I wanted to help Jim short term, but I knew I wasn't going to be the Quality Manager long term. I unleashed the quality team, and we instantly began making big improvements in the Quality Department. We made things happen with people that wanted to make things happen.

Jim came to me a few days later and said, *"See, I knew you could do it."* I said, *"I knew I could do it too. But, I also know I don't want to be doing it."* I informed Jim I had decided to stay a little longer. I told him I had hired a career consultant and was preparing to resign a few months later instead of resigning when my 30 day agreement with him was fulfilled. I wanted to be transparent to help him make better decisions moving forward. He needed to know I was leaving.

I began to plan my exit strategy with my career coach. I was extremely miserable during this time period because I was doing something I didn't want to be doing. That wasn't a good place to be as a leader. I was completely out of harmony. I could feel it and others could see it.

Jim Noreault modeled leadership. I watched him,

learned from him intentionally, and developed a desire to lead like him and impact people like he did. Jim left his mark on my life, and I'm grateful.

Three months after my 30 day promise to Jim was over, I walked into his office and resigned on August 15th, 2008. I was about to start my own Lean Consulting business, KaizenOps. A few years later, after shifting my focus from Lean Manufacturing to leadership development and after Ria had joined me, we changed the name of our business to Top Story Leadership.

It was hard to hand Jim my resignation that morning because of my respect for him and the strong relationship we had built. He took it and threw it in the trash, asking me to go home and reconsider. I did, only to return the next day with another copy. I had made my decision.

Jim is a great man. I still consider him a friend although we do not see each other or talk very often these days. But, I do get to see and speak to him occasionally. I will always remember the many lessons on leadership I learned from him. Thank you for your leadership Jim.

Kaizen is a Japanese word commonly used in Lean. It basically means continuous improvement. There are a few more translations such as: small change for the better and to take apart and put back together again with improvement. Therefore, KaizenOps translates to Continuous Improvement Operations.

One day in the fall of 2008 while driving to meet potential clients, which I had been doing for the past few months as I tried to get my Lean Manufacturing Consulting business going, I decided out of boredom to listen to an audio a friend of mine, Zac Sharrow, had given me nearly three years earlier.

When Zac gave it to me, I remember him saying, *"I thought you might like this audio. It's supposed to be a popular business book. My friend's dad said it was really good."*

Listening to the audio was the start of a major transformation in my life. I think about, talk about, and apply what I learned from that audio every day. It was a one-hour, condensed version of *The 7 Habits of Highly Effective People* by Stephen R. Covey.

I have decided *The 7 Habits* are like a hammer, and the other leadership books represent various types, sizes, and styles of nails each with a different purpose. If you are doing anything effectively, you are applying *The 7 Habits* whether you know it or not.

What would have been different if I had listened to the audio when I first received it three years earlier? A lot would have been different. Zac did not know how right he would be. I did more than like it. I loved it.

Listening to *The 7 Habits* literally caused me to transform my life. I will never forget Zac and always be grateful. He had no idea how big of an impact his small gesture would have on the rest of my life. Thanks for thinking of me Zac.

Near the start of the audio, Covey said, *"To truly learn this material, you must begin teaching it to others within 24-48 hours."* I took him at his word and have never stopped teaching what I learned from him.

I started applying the principles in my consulting business, during Lean training sessions, during Lean kaizen events, and during Lean Leadership Certification sessions. *The 7 Habits* quickly became, and remain, the foundation for everything I do.

I became more and more curious and started reading other books by Covey, his family, and numerous other personal growth and leadership development authors. I continued to teach and share all that I was learning with others. Although I didn't enjoy reading, when one book was finished, I would always start another.

The two pillars of Lean are *"Respect for the People"* and *"Continuous Improvement."* However, I teach them as two foundational layers with *Respect for the People* on the bottom supporting everything else. Most organizations applying Lean principles focus only on the *Continuous Improvement* layer of Lean and do very little training relative to people development. *Respect for the people* is about leadership development at all levels with all of the people regardless of their position or title. Very few organizations focus on this most critical layer or Lean.

Leadership development is the key to generating and sustaining the gains *continuous improvement* principles generate. Without formal professional leadership development training, most people will resist the changes created by Lean improvements. Leadership principles create a foundation that allows people to embrace, support, leverage, and lead change. When there is adequate leadership development training and leaders are modeling high impact leadership principles for the team, people become very engaged, proactive and highly effective.

True *respect for the people* is best achieved by creating an atmosphere of leadership at all levels. 360° of high impact, servant leadership is the key to creating a thriving and striving organization of any kind. But, when you are accelerating change with Lean transformation and initiatives, leadership development is usually the missing link when it comes to sustaining the gains.

Several years after introducing leadership materials

into my Lean training sessions, Elizabeth (Liz) Mendez, a Lean team member at a facility I was supporting, approached me with a book she had been reading. She handed it to me saying, *"It's The 17 Indisputable Laws of Teamwork by John Maxwell. You should read it. I think you will like it."*

I had asked her to read many books. Since Liz thought I should read it, I respected her judgment and read it. I was traveling from Alabama and was working in Texas at the time. I was in a hotel all week with nothing to do but read in the evenings. I read it in three days. I'm a slow reader, but I loved the book. When I told her I had finished it, she was surprised. She said I could keep it as a gift. She informed me she had another book for me to read too.

She proceeded to give me *The 21 Irrefutable Laws of Leadership* also by John Maxwell. My attraction to John and his teaching was strong after reading those two books. I was drawn to the principles Stephen Covey and John Maxwell were teaching.

Liz had no idea her generosity and thoughtfulness would lead me to launch myself to an entirely new level in the professional world of leadership development. Thank you for thinking of me Liz.

I didn't know it at the time, but my journey into the field of professional leadership training, coaching, and speaking was on the horizon. My influence would soon begin to extend beyond the blue-collar manufacturing industries as I began to gain influence across all industries.

18

DISCOVERING MY PURPOSE

The Start of My Leadership Journey

"When we are faced with change, we either step forward into growth, or we step backward into safety."
~ *Abraham Maslow*

Ria and I enjoy mountain biking. We raced in 2011 and 2012. Ria was the Alabama and Georgia State Champion in her class both years. She excels at everything she does. In late 2011, we were informed of a meeting to discuss constructing mountain bike trails locally at Chewacla State Park in Auburn, Alabama. We were excited. We only lived a mile from the park but had normally been driving 45 minutes or more to ride the nearest trails.

Ria and I met with the group and received permission from the Park Manager, O'Dell Banks, to begin constructing trails. We and about eight others started construction. In the coming months, we had more people joining to help out and were gaining momentum. However, O'Dell said we would need to halt new construction until we formed a formal organization to maintain and sustain the nearly 14 miles of trail we had completed in just under six months.

Our group decided to form an official chapter of the International Mountain Bicycling Association (IMBA). We were going to become the newest chapter of the Southern Off-Road Bicycling Association (SORBA). The name of our non-profit would be the Central

Alabama Mountain Pedalers (CAMP). Many members of the group expressed they wanted me to be the founding President. Ria and I had a long talk to determine if we wanted to sacrifice two years to grow and develop this startup organization.

After much thought, we decided to make the commitment together. She agreed to help and accepted the role of Secretary. It was time to assemble a team. We attracted many top notch people with natural leadership skills. We quickly filled the CAMP board with great people who valued helping others and making a positive difference in the community.

We were happy Philip Darden accepted the role of Vice-President. He had a passion for cycling and the outdoors. He possessed a very teachable spirit and wanted to learn more about leadership which, along with his natural leadership abilities, would make it easy for me to help grow, develop, and prepare him over the next few years. I expected he would take over the role as President when my two year term was complete.

CAMP membership quickly grew to 150 members. With Ria's help, we secured $10,000 and $100,000 Recreational Trails Program grants to purchase tools and further develop the trail system within the park. We built additional trails and features and made a significant impact on the amount of revenue the park was generating by increasing the number of visitors tremendously.

We held our first elections in the fall of 2013. As expected, Philip was elected to serve as the new CAMP President. He had done what good leaders do. He had built many relationships during his time as the CAMP VP which allowed him to easily fill the officer positions as others also completed their terms. He also added a few new positions. He was ready to continue to lead and live up to the CAMP motto *"We make things happen!"*

We are very proud of what Philip and the other CAMP leadership team members have accomplished as they continue to deliver outstanding results for the CAMP members, the state park, the community, and the visitors. The park will soon have nearly 25 total miles of new trails, many wooden features, and many more planned trails with dirt jumps and other expert features to be added later thanks to the volunteer efforts of CAMP. An amazing achievement in less than three years!

We are proud to have served with the CAMP team. It was the right time to do the right thing. We all made a contribution and a difference in our community.

Ria and I invested several thousand hours during those first two years to grow the organization, build relationships, and get results while building and growing a team to sustain the organization when we stepped aside. It was well worth our time. If you want to find out what kind of leader you are, lead a volunteer organization, especially one where the product is physical labor. We had a lot of fun and are excited they continue to grow, get results, and do well under Philip's leadership.

This was not the only thing we were doing during those two years. We were also busy growing ourselves and KaizenOps.

One morning in June 2012, I discovered an advertisement stating John Maxwell would be hosting his first ever *A Day About Books* event in Palm Beach, Florida in three weeks. I planned to be there.

"Coincidence is God's way of staying anonymous." ~ Les Brown

I had been thinking about writing my first book. I could not start a professional leadership development business teaching someone else's material. I needed my own. It was time.

Since age 19, Eric had been working with me as a Lean Manufacturing Consultant and had also become a student of leadership. He was now 21 and had already read many leadership books. So, I registered us both for the *A Day About Books* event with John Maxwell.

John was going to teach how he writes and publishes books. He should surely know a thing or two about the process. He has written and published many books over the past decades.

Eric and I made the long drive down and were excited to get to see and hear John. Entering the hotel, we saw a sign with the words *"Welcome John Maxwell Team!"* It was odd and somewhat confusing.

As we checked in, we were asked if we were with the John Maxwell Team (JMT). Assuming she wanted to know if we were there for the John Maxwell event, I answered, yes. She gave us a welcome letter. It stated there would be a reception later the same evening.

It seemed odd there was a reception for those attending the event the next day. We really didn't know what we didn't know because we had never attended any type of seminar or conference before. This was a first for us on all fronts. We decided to attend the reception in case we were supposed to be there.

As we walked up to the entrance, I told Eric, *"These people are connecting and seem much closer than you would expect a group of strangers to be."* He agreed as we made our way to the registration table where we were promptly asked if we were with the JMT. Again, we said yes because we thought we were. Our names could not be located, but a name tag was made for each of us, and we made our way into the energy filled crowd not knowing what to expect.

The first person we talked to asked, *"When did you join?"* We said we had not joined anything and were there for the *A Day About Books* event. He said, *"So, you're not a member?"* We said no and explained we did not understand why we received a letter saying we should be there and that we were further confused when the people at the registration table could not find our name on the list. We felt something wasn't right all along, but couldn't figure it out. It was slowly becoming clear. We were not supposed to be at the reception.

The gentleman proceeded to explain the JMT had started in August 2011, and it was John Maxwell's coaching, training, and speaking certification program. I said, *"We aren't supposed to be here. We are here by mistake. We should leave."* He said there was no need, invited us to stay, and continued to tell us about the program since we seemed interested. We were very interested. John had a certification program. My leadership development wheels were spinning as we continued to talk.

He was impressed by our knowledge of leadership principles. We have a natural ability to understand and retain leadership principles and love talking about leadership anytime anywhere with anyone. He said, *"You must meet Janice. She is a Coordinator."*

He shared our story with her and explained how we had accidentally ended up at the reception. She told us more about the program and explained how we could become certified members.

We ended the conversation with Janice saying, *"You did not end up here by accident. You are supposed to be here."* She was right, but I didn't know how right. I wanted to get certified. I already had a deep understanding of leadership principles. I thought learning more from John would accelerate my journey.

I remember thinking I was going to get certified and launch my professional leadership business. It was just the spark I needed to boost my confidence. Although looking back, I would have made it happen anyway. It wasn't as necessary as I thought at the time.

We had crashed the event by accident. But, it was no accident. The next day, John explained the program to the audience. He told us he was leaving his legacy, and the program was how he planned to do it. Once I found out the details, I registered both of us. We would be at John's next certification event in August 2012.

The certification would require many thousands of dollars of financial sacrifice. To say I was excited would be an understatement. It seemed to be one of those too good to be true deals. But, it was true. We could not believe it. We would be certified by John Maxwell to teach, speak, and coach in the area of leadership. We had to wait two long months for the certification event.

When the time came, we went and had a blast. We learned there was a higher level of the program for those wanting to go farther, the John Maxwell Mentorship Program. The Mentorship Program included a lot of focused coaching and mentoring. We made the decision quickly to enroll in this program too with many more thousands of dollars of financial sacrifice.

I had never made these types of significant financial sacrifices to develop myself or my family before. I was operating at a completely new level of awareness.

I left there with much thinking to do. I knew two things for sure. First, I was excited and couldn't wait for

Ria to get certified. Certifications happened twice a year at the time. So, we would have to wait for the next opportunity. Second, I was going to shift my focus from Lean Manufacturing to professional leadership development within all organizations across all industries.

I wanted to make a bigger and broader impact. At the end of 2012, I intentionally let my existing Lean contracts expire. Ria and I began to transform KaizenOps into Top Story Leadership with our primary focus on leadership development in all organizations while moving away from Lean Manufacturing Consulting.

Ria and I were happy when February 2013 arrived. I was excited for her. It was time for her to be certified, and I would be receiving additional training too. As a Mentorship Program member, I was able to receive new training while Ria was going through the standard certification training.

She enjoyed the experience, joined the Mentorship Program too, and was very excited about our future. Again, we were investing many tens of thousands of dollars to grow and develop ourselves professionally. We were on a mission.

Ria called my Mom at one of the breaks and said, *"JoAnne, you should come back in August with us! You will absolutely love this!"* Ria was fully onboard and wanted to get my Mom involved too.

Mom had seen my transformation accelerate and had started reading leadership books herself because of the positive changes she had seen in my life since 2008. Taking my mom back was a great idea. It didn't take long, and we had made our plans. The three of us were heading back to get mom certified in August 2013, and

Ria and I would get additional new training. Another round of financial sacrifices were made. We were constantly and consistently investing in ourselves in order to create the future we wanted for ourselves.

We had a couple of things to do before August. Ria and I had decided to host the Chick-fil-A Leadercast in Auburn, Alabama on May 10th, 2013.

We would be marketing Top Story Leadership as a resource for professional leadership development. We offered many complimentary training sessions as prizes to those attending. That event helped propel us forward. It gave us credibility and visibility which led to new relationships with many potential clients.

Before the August certification event, we were invited to participate in a very special leadership event with John Maxwell. There would be a major one week training event in Guatemala City, Guatemala, in June 2013. John, along with approximately 150 of us who had been certified, would begin the *"Transformation Begins with Me!"* cultural transformation initiative across the entire nation of Guatemala.

It was a great event with great success. Together, we trained over 20,000 Guatemalan leaders. We paid our expenses to get there, for our meals for the week, and for our hotel stay for the week. All of us were helping John help the Guatemalan people. We were no longer only investing in ourselves. We were now investing our time and money to truly help others.

We feel like we received much more than we gave. It was well worth our time and the financial investment we made to participate. It was an awesome week of teamwork. As John said, *"We made a difference with people that wanted to make a difference doing something that made a difference at a time that made a difference."*

DEFINING INFLUENCE

*"Only those who have learned the power of sincere and selfless
contribution experience life's deepest joy: true fulfillment."*
~ Tony Robbins

When August 2013 arrived, we experienced a great
week of growth. My mom absolutely loved it. She had
never experienced anything like the seminar. She's not
the only one. Most people haven't.

We all received tremendous value from the program
and have attended many other leadership development
seminars and conferences to intentionally learn from
various leadership development professionals.

*"The top 5% of achievers invest an average of $3,000 per year on
personal growth while the other 95% average only $7 per year."*
~ Les Brown

In 2012 and 2013, my growth was a priority. But, my
main focus became the growth and development of
others. I had achieved success far beyond my wildest
dreams in my Lean consulting business but was no
longer satisfied. I wanted to achieve more with and
through others. I was equipped to help others live their
dreams and achieve success. I was moving beyond
getting my own results and into the people
development phase of my leadership growth journey
where I would be helping other get better results.

Immediately after the February and August 2013
John Maxwell training sessions, Ria and I attended Les
Brown's speaker training seminar. We were sacrificing
and growing like crazy in many different ways with
many different people. We were living what we were
teaching. Valuing ourselves and investing in ourselves
over and over again.

The Les Brown trainings were something that gave us additional access to other top tier leadership and motivational speakers. It led to another amazing opportunity for Ria and ultimately me.

Ria won a speaking competition at the second training we attended with Les Brown. As one of the top five out of nearly 200 speakers in the room in August 2013, Ria received the chance to share the stage with Les Brown at some point in the future. This was an amazing opportunity for the winners. I was proud of her and could not wait for it to happen. A few months passed before we received the email from Les Brown's team: *"Be prepared to be in Los Angeles, California, on January 25th and 26th, 2014."* Again, we were ready to give up to go up.

We made the additional financial sacrifice and paid our own expenses to experience this very rare opportunity. We also had a speaking engagement setup in Anaheim, California, on January 21st, 2014. As a result, we enjoyed seeing and visiting much of the west coast in between our speaking engagements.

Saturday morning, January 25th arrived. It was time for the pre-meeting with Les. Those speaking with Les would be discussing the details of the weekend with him. Ria was the only speaker with a family member there for support. I stayed with her while everyone was waiting for Les to arrive. Once he did, he asked those in the room to tell him what they would be speaking about.

After everyone finished, he looked at me and said, *"Who are you?"* I explained who I was and why I was there. I let him know I didn't want to abuse my privilege and would be happy to leave if necessary since I was not one of the invited speakers. Les instantly said,

"Oh, yes you are! You're not getting away that easy. You're going on stage too."

I was not about to pass up this once in a lifetime chance. No matter what, I was ready to jump off the cliff and grow my wings on the way down. The thought of saying no was in my mind for only a fraction of a second. Everyone else had known they would be speaking and had been working on their speeches for months. I didn't expect Les to ask me to speak. I accepted his generous offer without hesitation and without time to prepare a speech. I would simply make it happen.

I simply said, *"Okay! Thank you sir!"* I knew I could be authentic and easily speak about leadership principles as they related to my life. I also knew I could be funny, especially being from Alabama with a strong southern accent, talking to people in Los Angeles.

Ria and the others did an amazing job. They were very polished and appeared as though they had been doing this for years. I was the last speaker on Sunday afternoon. The thoughts I planned to share would fit well with closing down the event.

I started my talk by asking them, *"How many of y'all are from the L.A. area?"* After most raised their hands, I said, *"How many of y'all can tell I'm not."* They laughed pretty loud. I was connecting. Then, I followed with a few lines to poke fun at my heavy southern accent. I am from the Deep South, Alabama. You're likely to realize it when you hear the first syllable out of my mouth.

Next, I said, *"Before I get started, you should know I'm bilingual. I don't say it to impress you, but to warn you. Yep, I speak two languages: English and country."* That got another big laugh. I went on to tell them, *"I sometimes speak both at the same time, and you'll know when I do because you won't be able to understand a word I'm saying."* That brought more laughter. I was off to a great start and continued with the rest of my speech. If you're willing to be yourself, it's pretty easy.

Les came up and joined me as I finished. He repeated my bilingual joke and laughed hysterically along with the audience. He said he liked my sincerity and wanted to work with me to further develop my speaking skills. I stepped out on the limb, but it didn't break. I had his approval. Les was outstanding the entire weekend. He offered to personally mentor us and to write the foreword for any books we were writing if we were interested.

Experiencing the private mentoring sessions with Les during our visit was awesome. I had the opportunity to share the stage with Les Brown too.

You must believe in yourself. Then, you must develop yourself. But, in the end, you *must* bet on yourself. You must be prepared for the opportunity when it presents itself.

"It is better to be prepared for an opportunity and not have one than it is to have an opportunity and not be prepared."
~ Les Brown

Hopefully, sharing a short version of my personal leadership journey has helped you better understand the principles you've been reading about. I have not always been where I am today. I started changing the way I thought, which changed the way I felt, which changed what I did. I started making different choices that allowed me to get different results.

Tomorrow, I will no longer be where I am today.

DEFINING INFLUENCE

*"The mind is the master-weaver, both of the inner garment of
character and the outer garment of circumstance."*
~ James Allen

Read Allen's words several times slowly, thinking
deeply about what you have learned about your
influence. Where are you? Where do you want to be?
Consider how his words relate to your personal story?
Your future? And, your journey?

19

CONCLUSION

Make It Happen or Someone Else Will

"If you do what is easy, your life will be hard. But if you do what is hard, your life will be easy." ~ Les Brown

I hope you believe, as I do, everyone is a leader. We all have influence. We all are on the leadership scale. As leaders, we must grow and develop our influence while using it to positively impact ourselves and others.

You should have a much higher level of awareness about the value of influence and fully understand: Leadership is influence. Nothing more. Nothing less.

Stop and Think: How will your life change if you increase your influence a little? What will get better? What will be different?

Stop and Think: How will your life change if you increase your influence a lot? What will get better? What will be different?

Stop and Think: What are the three most important things you need to stop doing? Big or small?

1. _____

2. _____

3. _____

Stop and Think: What are the three most important things you need to start doing? Big or small?

1. _____

2. _____

3. _____

I hope you stopped, reflected on what you have learned, thought deeply about increasing your influence, and wrote down several action items. If you didn't take the time to reflect, when will you do it? If not now, when? I cannot change your life. I cannot make it better. You must take action.

My goal has been to attempt to answer the five questions I posed at the start. Let's revisit them to bring them back into your thoughts:

1. **Why do we influence?** Our character determines our intent and *why* we influence ourselves and others. Who we are on the inside is what matters. Who we are on the inside determines what people see, feel, and experience on the outside. When it comes to character, our *intent* is our *"first impression."*

Intent is the foundation of trust. Our intent determines if others will allow us the opportunity to build trust with them. Our choices will develop or destroy our character. Who we are determines why we do what we do. Our character is revealed through our intent.

2. *How* **do we influence?** Our character combined with our competency determines *how* we influence ourselves and others. Who we are and what we know creates our unique style of influence.

Trust is the foundation of influence (leadership). The level of trust we build with others determines how much influence we have with them. We cannot make people trust us. We can only choose to be trustworthy. Who we are (character) is the primary component of trust. What we know (competency) is the secondary component of trust. We must be proactive and take responsibility in order to build and sustain trust.

3. *Where* **do we influence?** Our passion leads us to our purpose and ultimately determines *where* we will have the greatest influence with ourselves and others. What motivates and inspires us gives us the energy and authenticity to motivate and inspire others.

We must become intentional about leading ourselves based on our passion. Our passion fueled by our purpose gives us unmatched energy. The fire burning within us energizes, motivates, and inspires others with similar interests. Our greatest impact is in our passion and purpose zone.

4. *Who* **do we influence?** We influence those *who* buy-in to us and believe in us. Only those valuing and seeking what we value and seek will volunteer to follow us. They will give us or deny us permission to influence them based on how well we have developed our character and competency.

We will have the greatest influence with those like us. Who we are is who we attract. This attraction is based on our character primarily and our competency secondarily. If we want to attract people to us with well-developed character, we must develop our own character to an equal or higher level. We must value and develop the character traits we seek in others. We must go first. We cannot wait.

5. **When do we influence?** We influence others *when* they want to be influenced. Just as we get to choose when others have influence with us, others have the same choice and get to decide when to accept or reject our influence.

No matter who we are or what we know, we will not be able to influence others until they want to be influenced. They must have the desire to grow and change before they will consider our influence. This is a choice they must make. They must want it on the inside before they will search for it on the outside. We must continually grow and develop ourselves, so others will seek our influence when they are ready to change.

I strongly encourage you to continue growing and developing your mind by continuing to read leadership development and personal growth books. I have referenced many that have helped me on my journey. However, there are thousands more out there. I have also published many more since publishing *Defining Influence* in 2014.

I would like to thank you for allowing me the opportunity to potentially influence you and to inspire you to make positive changes in your life.

I hope you will share all you've learned about leadership with others and help me transform this world we live in from what it is to what it can be. Remember, *"Transformation Begins with Me!"* We must be the change we want to see in others. If not you, who? If not now, when?

FEEDBACK

I welcome hearing how this book has influenced the way you think, the way you sell, or the results you have achieved because of what you've learned in it. Please feel free to share your thoughts with me by email at:

Mack@MackStory.com

To order my books, audio books and other resources, please visit: TopStoryLeadership.com or Amazon.

ABOUT THE AUTHOR

Mack's story is an amazing journey of personal and professional growth. He married Ria in 2001. He has one son, Eric, born in 1991.

After graduating high school in 1987, Mack joined the United States Marine Corps Reserve as an 0311 infantryman. Soon after, he began his 20 plus year manufacturing career. Graduating with highest honors, he earned an Executive Bachelor of Business Administration degree from Faulkner University.

Mack began his career in manufacturing in 1988 on the front lines of a large production machine shop. He eventually grew himself into upper management and found his niche in lean manufacturing and along with it, developed his passion for leadership. In 2008, he launched his own Lean Manufacturing and Leadership Development firm.

From 2005-2012, Mack led leaders and their cross-functional teams through more than 11,000 hours of process improvement, organizational change, and cultural transformation. Ria joined Mack full-time in late 2013.

In 2013, they worked with John C. Maxwell as part of an international training event focused on the Cultural Transformation in Guatemala where over 20,000 leaders were trained. They also shared the stage with internationally recognized motivational speaker Les Brown in 2014.

Mack and Ria have published 20+ books on personal growth and leadership development and publish more each year. In 2018, they reached 66,000 international followers on LinkedIn where they provide daily motivational, inspirational, and leadership content to people all over the world.

Clients: ATD (Association for Talent Development), Auburn University, Chevron, Chick-fil-A, Kimberly Clark, Koch Industries, Southern Company, and the U.S. Military.

Mack is an inspiration for people everywhere as an example of achievement, growth, and personal development. His passion motivates and inspires people all over the world!

WHAT WE OFFER:

- ✓ Keynote Speaking: Conferences, Seminars, Onsite
- ✓ Workshops: Onsite/Offsite Half/Full/Multi Day
- ✓ Leadership Development Support: Leadership, Teamwork, Personal Growth, Organizational Change, Planning, Executing, Trust, Cultural Transformation, Communication, Time Management, Selling with Character, Resilience, & Relationship Building
- ✓ Blue-Collar Leadership® Development
- ✓ Corporate Retreats
- ✓ Women's Retreat (with Ria Story)
- ✓ Limited one-on-one coaching/mentoring
- ✓ On-site Lean Leadership Certification
- ✓ Lean Leader Leadership Development
- ✓ Become licensed to teach our content

FOR MORE INFORMATION PLEASE VISIT:

BlueCollarLeadership.com
TopStoryLeadership.com

FOLLOW US ON SOCIAL MEDIA:

LinkedIn.com/in/MackStory
Facebook.com/Mack.Story

LinkedIn.com/in/RiaStory
Facebook.com/Ria.Story

LISTEN/SUBSCRIBE TO OUR PODCASTS AT:

Mack Story: Anchor.fm/BlueCollarLeadership
Ria Story: Anchor.fm/RiaStory

Excerpt from

10 Values of High Impact Leaders

Our values are the foundation upon which we build our character. I'll be sharing 10 values high impact leaders work to master because they know these values will have a tremendous impact on their ability to lead others well. You may be thinking, *"Aren't there more than 10 leadership values?"* Absolutely! They seem to be endless. And, they are all important. These are simply 10 key values which I have chosen to highlight.

Since leadership is very dynamic and complex, the more values you have been able to internalize and utilize synergistically together, the more effective you will be. The more influence you will have.

"High performing organizations that continuously invest in leadership development are now defining new 21st century leadership models to deal with today's gaps in their leadership pipelines and the new global business environment. These people-focused organizations have generated nearly 60% improved business growth, reported a 66% improvement in bench strength, and showed a 62% improvement in employee retention. And, our research shows that it is not enough to just spend money on leadership training, but rather to follow specific practices that drive accelerated business results." ~ Josh Bersin

Do you want to become a high impact leader?

I believe everyone is a leader, but they are leading at different levels.

I believe everyone can and should lead from *where they are.*

I believe everyone can and should make a high impact.

I believe growth doesn't just happen; we must make it happen.

I believe before you will invest in yourself you must first believe in yourself.

I believe leaders must believe in their team before they will invest in their team.

I truly believe *everything rises and falls on influence.*

There is a story of a tourist who paused for a rest in a small town in the mountains. He went over to an old man sitting on a bench in front of the only store in town and inquired, *"Friend, can you tell me something this town is noted for?"*

"Well," replied the old man, *"I don't rightly know except it's the starting point to the world. You can start here and go anywhere you want."* [1]

That's a great little story. We are all at *"the starting point"* to the world, and we *"can start here and go anywhere we want."* We can expand our influence 360° in all directions by starting in the center with ourselves.

Consider the following illustration. Imagine you are standing in the center. You can make a high impact. However, it will not happen by accident. You must become intentional. You must live with purpose while focusing on your performance as you develop your potential.

Note: Illustration and 10 Values are listed on the following pages.

Why we do what we do is about our *purpose.*

How we do what we do is about our *performance.*

What we do will determine our *potential.*

Where these three components overlap, you will achieve a
HIGH IMPACT.

10 Values of High Impact Leaders

1
THE VALUE OF VISION
Vision is the foundation of hope.
"When there's hope in the future, there's power in the present." ~ Les Brown

2
THE VALUE OF MODELING
Someone is always watching you.
"Who we are on the inside is what people see on the outside." ~ Mack Story

3
THE VALUE OF RESPONSIBILITY
When we take responsibility, we take control.
"What is common sense is not always common practice." ~ Stephen R. Covey

4
THE VALUE OF TIMING
It matters when you do what you do.
"It's about doing the right thing for the right reason at the right time." ~ Mack Story

5

THE VALUE OF RESPECT
To be respected, we must be respectful.
"Go See, ask why, and show respect"
~ Jim Womack

6

THE VALUE OF EMPOWERMENT
Leaders gain influence by
giving it to others.
"Leadership is not reserved for leaders."
~ Marcus Buckingham

7

THE VALUE OF DELEGATION
We should lead with questions
instead of directions.
"Delegation 101: Delegating 'what to do,' makes
you responsible. Delegating 'what to
accomplish,' allows others to become
responsible."
~ Mack Story

8

THE VALUE OF MULTIPLICATION
None of us is as influential as all of us.
"To add growth, lead followers. To multiply,
lead leaders." ~ John C. Maxwell

9

THE VALUE OF RESULTS
Leaders like to make things happen.
"Most people fail in the getting started."
~ Maureen Falcone

10

THE VALUE OF SIGNIFICANCE
Are you going to settle for success?
"Significance is a choice that only successful people can make."
~ Mack Story

Order books online at Amazon or

TopStoryLeadership.com

High impact leaders align their habits with key values in order to maximize their influence. High impact leaders intentionally grow and develop themselves in an effort to more effectively grow and develop others.

These *10 Values* are commonly understood. However, they are not always commonly practiced. These *10 Values* will help you build trust and accelerate relationship building. Those mastering these *10 Values* will be able to lead with speed as they develop 360° of influence from wherever they are.

Order books online at Amazon or TopStoryLeadership.com

10 Foundational Elements of Intentional Transformation serves as a source of motivation and inspiration to help you climb your way to the next level and beyond as you learn to intentionally create a better future for yourself. The pages will ENCOURAGE, ENGAGE, and EMPOWER you as you become more focused and intentional about moving from where you are to where you want to be.

All of us are somewhere, but most of us want to be somewhere else. However, we don't always know how to get there. You will learn how to intentionally move forward as you learn to navigate the 10 foundational layers of transformation.

Order books online at Amazon or TopStoryLeadership.com

"Sales persuasion and influence, moving others, has changed more in the last 10 years than it has in the last 100 years. It has transitioned from buyer beware to seller beware" ~ Daniel Pink

So, it's no longer *"Buyer beware!"* It's *"Seller beware!"* Why? Today, the buyer has the advantage over the seller. Most often, they are holding it in their hand. It's a smart phone. They can learn everything about your product before they meet you. They can compare features and prices instantly. The major advantage you do still have is: YOU! IF they like you. IF they trust you. IF they feel you want to help them.

This book is filled with 30 short chapters providing unique insights that will give you the advantage, not over the buyer, but over your competition: those who are selling what you're selling. It will help you sell yourself.

Order books online at Amazon or BlueCollarLeadership.com

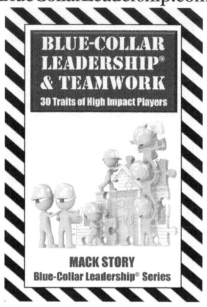

Are you ready to play at the next level and beyond?

In today's high stakes game of business, the players on the team are the competitive advantage for any organization. But, only if they are on the field instead of on the bench.

The competitive advantage for every individual is developing 360° of influence regardless of position, title, or rank.

Blue-Collar Leadership® & Teamwork provides a simple, yet powerful and unique, resource for individuals who want to increase their influence and make a high impact. It's also a resource and tool for leaders, teams, and organizations, who are ready to Engage the Front Line to Improve the Bottom Line.

Order books online at Amazon or BlueCollarLeadership.com

"I wish someone had given me these books 30 years ago when I started my career on the front lines. They would have changed my life then. They can change your life now." ~ Mack Story

Blue-Collar Leadership® & Supervision and *Blue-Collar Leadership®* are written specifically for those who lead the people on the frontlines and for those on the front lines. With 30 short, easy to read 3 page chapters, these books contain powerful, yet simple to understand leadership lessons.

Note: These two Blue-Collar Leadership® books are the blue-collar version of the MAXIMIZE books and contain nearly identical content.

Down load the first 5 chapters of each book FREE at:
BlueCollarLeadership.com

Order books online at Amazon or BlueCollarLeadership.com

The biggest challenge in process improvement and cultural transformation isn't identifying the problems. It's execution: implementing and sustaining the solutions.

Blue-Collar Kaizen is a resource for anyone in any position who is, or will be, leading a team through process improvement and change. Learn to engage, empower, and encourage your team for long term buy-in and sustained gains.

Mack Story has over 11,000 hours experience leading hundreds of leaders and thousands of their cross-functional kaizen team members through process improvement, organizational change, and cultural transformation. He shares lessons learned from his experience and many years of studying, teaching, and applying leadership principles.

Order books online at Amazon or TopStoryLeadership.com

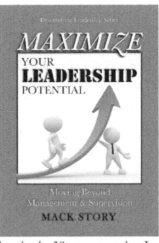

"I wish someone had given me these books 30 years ago when I started my career. They would have changed my life then. They can change your life now." ~ Mack Story

MAXIMIZE Your Potential will help you learn to lead yourself well. *MAXIMIZE Your Leadership Potential* will help you learn to lead others well. With 30 short, easy to read 3 page chapters, these books contain simple and easy to understand, yet powerful leadership lessons.

Note: These two MAXIMIZE books are the white-collar, or non-specific, version of the Blue-Collar Leadership® books and contain nearly identical content.

ABOUT RIA STORY

Mack's wife, Ria, is also a motivational leadership speaker, author, and a world class coach who has a unique ability to help people develop and achieve their life and career goals, and guide them in building the habits and discipline to achieve their personal view of greatness. Ria brings a wealth of personal experience in working with clients to achieve their personal goals and aspirations in a way few coaches can.

Like many, Ria has faced adversity in life. Raised on an isolated farm in Alabama, she suffered extreme sexual abuse by her father from age 12 to 19. Desperate to escape, she left home at 19 without a job, a car, or even a high school diploma. Ria learned to be resilient, and not just survive, but thrive. (Watch her 7 minute TEDx talk at RiaStory.com/TEDx) She worked her way through school, acquiring an MBA with a 4.0 GPA, and eventually resigned from her career in the corporate world to pursue a passion for helping others achieve success.

Ria's background includes more than 10 years in healthcare administration, including several years in management, and later, Director of Compliance and Regulatory Affairs for a large healthcare organization. Ria's responsibilities included oversight of thousands of organizational policies, organizational compliance with all State and Federal regulations, and responsibility for several million dollars in Medicare appeals.

Ria co-founded Top Story Leadership, which offers leadership speaking, training, coaching, and consulting.

Ria's Story From Ashes To Beauty
by Ria Story

The unforgettable story and inspirational memoir of a young woman who was extremely sexually abused by her father from age 12 to 19 and then rejected by her mother. (Watch 7 minutes of her story in her TEDx talk at RiaStory.com/TEDx)

For the first time, Ria publicly reveals details of the extreme sexual abuse she endured growing up. 13 years after leaving home at 19, she decided to speak out about her story and encourage others to find hope and healing.

Determined to not only survive, but also thrive, Ria shares how she was able to overcome the odds and find hope and healing to Achieve Abundant Life. She shares the leadership principles she applied to find professional success, personal significance, and details how she was able to find the courage to share her story to give hope to others around the world.

Ria states, *"It would be easier for me to let this story go untold forever and simply move on with life...One of the most difficult things I've ever done is write this book. Victims of sexual assault or abuse don't want to talk because they want to avoid the social stigma and the fear of not being believed or the possibility of being blamed for something that was not their fault. My hope and prayer is someone will benefit from learning how I was able to overcome such difficult circumstances. That brings purpose to the pain and reason enough to share what I would rather have left behind forever. Our scars make us stronger."*

Available at Amazon.com in paperback, audio, and eBook. To order your signed copy, to learn more about Ria, or to book her to speak at your event, please visit:
RiaStory.com/TEDx

Order books online at Amazon or RiaStory.com

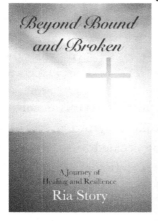

Ria's Story
From Ashes To Beauty

Ria Story

In *Beyond Bound and Broken*, Ria shares how she overcame the shame, fear, and doubt she developed after enduring years of extreme sexual abuse by her father. Forced to play the role of a wife and even shared with other men due to her father's perversions, Ria left home at 19 without a job, a car, or even a high-school diploma. This book also contains lessons on resilience and overcoming adversity that you can apply to your own life.

In *Ria's Story From Ashes To Beauty*, Ria tells her personal story of growing up as a victim of extreme sexual abuse from age 12 – 19, leaving home to escape, and her decision to tell her story. She shares her heart in an attempt to help others overcome their own adversity.

Order books online at Amazon or RiaStory.com

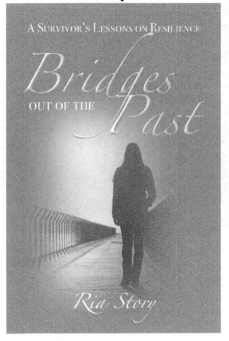

It's not what happens to you in life. It's who you become because of it. We all experience pain, grief, and loss in life. Resilience is the difference between *"I didn't die,"* and *"I learned to live again."* In this captivating book on resilience, Ria walks you through her own horrific story of more than seven years of sexual abuse by her father. She then shares how she learned not only to survive, but also to thrive in spite of her past. Learn how to overcome challenges, obstacles, and adversity in your own life by building a bridge out of the past and into the future.

(Watch 7 minutes of her story at RiaStory.com/TEDx)

Order books online at Amazon or RiaStory.com

Note: Leadership Gems is the generic, non-gender specific, version of Leadership Gems for Women. The content is very similar.

Women are naturally high level leaders because they are relationship oriented. However, it's a *"man's world"* out there and natural ability isn't enough to help you be successful as a leader. You must be intentional.

Ria packed these books with 30 leadership gems which very successful people internalize and apply. Ria has combined her years of experience in leadership roles of different organizations along with years of studying, teaching, training, and speaking on leadership to give you these 30, short and simple, yet powerful and profound, lessons to help you become very successful, regardless of whether you are in a formal leadership position or not.

Order books online at Amazon or RiaStory.com

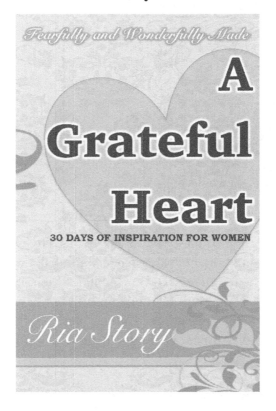

Become inspired by this 30-day collection of daily devotions for women, where you will find practical advice on intentionally living with a grateful heart, inspirational quotes, short journaling opportunities, and scripture from God's Word on practicing gratitude.

Order books online at Amazon or RiaStory.com

Ria's *Effective Leadership Series* books are written to develop and enhance your leadership skills, while also helping you increase your abilities in areas like communication and relationships, time management, planning and execution, leading and implementing change. Look for more books in the *Effective Leadership Series*:

- *Straight Talk: The Power of Effective Communication*

- *PRIME Time: The Power of Effective Planning*

- *Change Happens: Leading Yourself and Others through Change (Co-authored by Ria & Mack Story)*

255

Made in the USA
Columbia, SC
03 March 2019